Now That You Are a Catholic

REVISED AND EXPANDED EDITION

D1425155

Now That You Are a Catholic

*An Informal Guide to Catholic
Customs, Traditions and Practices*

REVISED AND EXPANDED EDITION

John J. Kenny, C.S.P.

Paulist Press
New York/Mahwah, N.J.

Cover design by Bright i Design

All Scripture extracts are taken from the New Revised Standard Version, copyright © 1989, by the Division of Christian Education of the National Council of the Churches of Christ in the United States of America and reprinted by permission of the publisher.

Library of Congress Cataloging-in-Publication Data

Kenny, John J., 1931–
    Now that you are a Catholic : an informal guide to Catholic customs, traditions and practices / John J. Kenny.—Rev. and expanded ed.
        p.   cm.
    ISBN 0-8091-4194-9 (alk. paper)
    1. Christian life—Catholic authors.   2. Catholic Church—Doctrines.
I. Title.
BX2350.3 .K46 2003
248.4′82—dc21

2003010485

Published by Paulist Press
997 Macarthur Boulevard
Mahwah, New Jersey 07430

www.paulistpress.com

Printed and bound in the
United States of America

Introduction

Easter is over.

You've just been baptized or made your profession of Catholic faith. Congratulations! You may have had to face opposition from old friends and relatives. Perhaps even some Catholics did not quite understand: "Why would anyone become a Catholic when the Church is such a mess?"

But *you* focused on the important things. You know that the Church in its long history has gone through alternating periods of rest and unrest. It's a human institution and we expect that of anything human. But God saved us through the human nature of his Son and he continues his saving work through a human community of believers, the Church. He has called you to be a part of his community. We are human, you and I, and we are the Church.

This little book is not designed to give you more insight into the beliefs and history of the Catholic Church. You have a lifetime to explore the wonderland of belief and to examine the common ground on which the people of God have been wayfaring for centuries.

This book is designed to help you find your place in the community of believers as easily and conveniently as possible. You are already aware that the Church is a human family. It has customs, traditions and practices such as any large family or community has. Much of all this is related to Catholic belief, but much of it is just this family's way of doing things.

Lifetime Catholics have picked it up from parents, parochial school, Catholic friends and neighbors over a period of years, and it has become part of them. This is the easy way to learn. But this also makes it hard for a lifetime Catholic to separate what is essential from what is not. He or she may be shaken when an old tradition dies or when a familiar practice changes abruptly.

This book is a practical guide to the way things are done in the American Church. These are not necessarily the best ways; they do not come from some eternal decree of God. But you will want to know them and thus be able to thread your way through the maze. You will then be free to work at the serious (and, hopefully, joyous) business of being a Christian in this world and be able to profit most from what your religion has to offer.

The first part of the book is a series of "how-to" sections: "Going to Mass," "Getting Married" and so on. The second part explains terms used in the American Church. Many of these terms refer to older practices familiar to lifetime Catholics. Some of the practices may never affect your life, but you will want to know what they are. There are also some newer terms that reflect the changes of the past forty years. The Appendix includes some of the common prayers, the Ten Commandments and the Beatitudes.

May you find all this helpful as you learn to know and love the Church, that community of which Jesus spoke when he said: "By this everyone will know that you are my disciples, if you have love for one another" (John 13:35).

Part I

1
Joining a Parish

The Rite of Christian Initiation for Adults (RCIA) has introduced a rich pattern of informational, social and liturgical introduction to Catholic parish life. With the help of sponsors, the RCIA team and the parish community, you've come to know your parish. Even if you were received into the Catholic Church with a simpler or less formal process, you know what your parish is.

But for you it may be graduation time and you are leaving that warm campus ministry community. Or that great job offer has come through and you are moving to another state. How do you find a new parish? You may be surprised to learn that the Catholic Church has already selected a parish for you.

"Who, me? I thought I had a choice!" You do, really. But ordinarily Catholics are expected to join the parish within whose boundaries they reside. You should know that the Roman Catholic Church has divided the whole world into territorial sections called *dioceses*, each presided over by a bishop. These dioceses have been subdivided into territorial units called *parishes*, each presided over by a pastor. Certain religious functions such as baptisms, weddings and funerals are ordinarily reserved to parishes. It's not as neat and tidy as it seems. There are exceptions that complicate the pattern.

Take *national* parishes. In the United States many parishes were originally established to serve ethnic groups rather than everybody within specified territorial boundaries. This was necessary to take care of the large numbers of immigrants who came from Europe during the nineteenth and early twentieth centuries. Though the Mass was said in Latin, sermons, announcements and parish business were done in Polish, Italian, Slovak or German.

Many of the national parishes have become territorial parishes or have closed down. But you may still find a Lithuanian or French national parish (or, currently, a Spanish parish) where some or all of the Masses are celebrated in the language of the ethnic group. If you are a member of that ethnic group you may substitute the national parish for your territorial parish, and have full access to the adopted parish for the purposes usually reserved by the territorial parish (i.e., baptism, marriage, funerals, etc.).

The university parish is a recent development. If you are a student or teacher at certain universities, you can become a member of the parish established specifically for the university community. Of course, a student or teacher may choose to remain a member of a territorial parish.

Many university religious centers are not parishes, though they may perform certain parish functions. In some urban centers you may also find a liturgical community associated with the chapel of a religious order.

A further complication: A million Catholics in the United States belong to the Eastern rites of the Church. The people who belong to Eastern rite parishes have bishops of their own whose dioceses may cover a very large section of the United States. The ancestors of these people came from Eastern Europe, especially Ukraine, and from the Near East, especially Lebanon. Words like Byzantine Rite, Ruthenian, Greek Catholic, Maronite or Melkite identify these groups.

You are welcome to attend Mass and receive Communion in these churches. But, thanks to a quirk of history, you are not supposed to join one of these parishes unless you were received into the Catholic Church by a priest of an Eastern rite. Such churches are easily confused with the independent Eastern Churches such as the Greek Orthodox Church or the Armenian Church.

At this point, you may feel the need for a rule of thumb. This one has the advantage of simplicity: Unless you are associated with a university or have a strong ethnic attachment, the logical move is to try the local territorial parish first. The great majority of American Catholics goes to Mass, receive the sacraments and participate in religious activities of the parish in which they live.

By asking a Catholic neighbor or by calling up the parish office, you can find out what times Mass is celebrated. At Mass you will receive a bulletin that lists the names of the parish staff, times of Mass, times of other religious services and the parish activities for the week.

You may want to register officially in the parish. Most parishes have a register of parishioners and an envelope system for church contributions. The envelope system is a convenience for the parish, but it also will help you at income tax time.

As far as financial support is concerned, be generous. Figure out what a fair share would be and give a bit more if you can. Some parishes have a large debt or may be operating a parochial school. The health of a parish community depends to a great extent on the generosity of its responsible parishioners.

Registering in the parish may give you an opportunity to meet your parish priests. You can telephone the rectory and make an appointment. Priests enjoy meeting a new parishioner, particularly a convert. And the priest may prove to be a real help in your adjustment to parish life.

But what if plunging in seems too much all at once? Then feel no immediate obligation to immerse yourself in parish activities. Furthermore, if you should find that you are not at home in the local parish for some reason, you owe no one an explanation. As a Catholic, you are free to attend Mass wherever you want. The essential thing is for you to find a community where you can join joyously in liturgical celebration. If you have to go outside your territorial parish to achieve this, go where your spirit is best nourished. Then any parish involvement will grow out of the sense of Christian community nurtured by this shared eucharistic experience.

2

Going to Mass

The Last Supper was a simple gathering. Its significant words and gestures could be done in a few minutes. We are not surprised to learn that over the centuries the Church has developed this simple rite into a much more elaborate ceremony. But the Mass remains what it always was. The Church does what Jesus did at the Last Supper: It celebrates the first coming, the life, death, resurrection and second coming of God's only Son. This chapter is written not to help you gain more insight into the significance of the Mass, but to help you with the many details involved in the way it is celebrated today.

As a beginning, it is good to plan to arrive early for Mass, but not so early that you find the parking lot filled with cars from an earlier Mass. Getting to church about ten minutes before Mass is just about right.

On entering the church, most Catholics dip the fingertips of their hand into the holy water font and make the sign of the cross. This is a traditional reminder of baptism and the Christian's new life in Christ.

Where do you sit? In Catholic churches it is rare to find any pews reserved. You can choose anyone you like. The front quarter of the church offers the best opportunity for full participation in the Mass. If you are concerned about when to stand, sit or kneel, you can avoid the first row or two and count on watching the movements of somebody in front of you who looks confidently Catholic. If you are worried about disturbances from your children, you can see if the church has a "crying room." Of course, normal restlessness on the part of children should be expected by priest and people. A crying room is primarily for those whose children are too young to avoid memorable disturbances.

In most churches it is customary to genuflect before entering a pew. You touch your knee to the floor as kind of a bow to Jesus, present in the Eucharist. In many newer churches, the tabernacle containing the Eucharist will not be near the center and people may not genuflect. It is still customary when passing the tabernacle, wherever it is, to genuflect or at least bow the head reverently. You may see some people making the sign of the cross and striking their breast while genuflecting. This is not necessary.

On entering a pew, Catholics usually kneel in prayer a few moments before sitting down. This can help you prepare for worship. It can also be hard on the knees if you don't check the kneeler. It should be swung down to provide a proper surface for tender shinbones. Do not be surprised to see people who arrive late pausing to kneel down even though the rest of the congregation is standing or sitting. Some modern Catholic churches do not have kneelers; in this case it is appropriate to sit down right away.

You probably will find a Mass book awaiting you in the pew. Such booklets are of limited usefulness. Designed to permit the congregation to read every word of the Mass, they can divert people from spontaneous participation in the liturgy. What you need from the booklet are the words of hymns, the Gloria and the Nicene Creed. Hymns are no problem because they are announced by number and page. The Gloria and the Nicene Creed are found in the first pages of text and do not require strenuous hunting down.

You can learn all the other prayers and responses by listening to them and perhaps repeating them quietly just a bit behind the rest of the congregation. Trying to do everything "by the book" is distracting. If the booklet fascinates you, it is no crime to borrow it. At home you can go over what was done at Mass if you find that helpful.

Unless you always attend Mass in the same church with the same priest, you can expect some variety in the way things are done. If a Mass is labeled "youth" or "contemporary" in the parish bulletin, you can expect it to be livelier than the customary Mass. Styles of music and song vary considerably from parish to parish and sometimes even from Mass to Mass.

Usually an entrance hymn greets the priest and his assistants as they enter the church. The people stand to sing as the priest approaches the altar. Sometimes there is no music or hymn. And in some places, the priest has no assistants and is alone on the altar until Communion is distributed. You will soon discover what is customary in your parish.

There is no reason to feel conspicuous if you hesitate before following the standing, sitting and kneeling of the congregation. Only you will know that you are responding hesitantly. The naturally slow risers, sitters and kneelers will make your actions seem quite timely. The reason for standing, sitting or kneeling will become apparent as you get familiar with the procedures of the Mass.

After a brief introductory rite, which includes an admission of sin, the Gloria and the prayer of the day, the Mass proceeds into its two main parts: the Liturgy of the Word of God and the Liturgy of the Eucharist.

The Liturgy of the Word of God comes first. In it, God's Word comes to the congregation through readings from the Bible and in the sermon. The people respond to God's Word in ways that will slip naturally into your memory.

To elaborate a bit, at Sunday Masses there are three readings from the Bible. The first is most often from the Old Testament, the second from any part of the New Testament other than the Gospels, and the third from one of the four Gospels. A layperson called a "lector" usually does the first two readings while the people remain seated. The congregation recites or sings the responses.

The people stand during the reading of the Gospel. Standing serves as an expression of respect for the words and life of Jesus. The priest or deacon and the congregation make a gesture at the beginning of the reading: A small sign of the cross is made with the thumb on the forehead, mouth and breast. It is a prayer that God will impress the words of the Gospel on our minds, on our lips and in our hearts. The sermon, called a *homily,* follows. The people's response usually is the Nicene Creed, a fifth-century formulation of Catholic belief. Next comes the Prayer of the Faithful or the Bidding Prayers, prayers for the needs of the Church, the world and the local community. On some occasions, in some parishes, the people add their own spontaneous prayer petitions. The Prayer of the Faithful concludes the Liturgy of the Word of God.

The Liturgy of the Eucharist follows. The Eucharist is simply doing what Jesus did at the Last Supper. Everything else is the current form of liturgical elaboration.

The offertory comes first. During this time, the bread (usually shaped into small discs called *hosts*), the wine and water are brought to the altar. A hymn is usually sung and the collection is taken up. The offertory includes the setting of the table for the Eucharist.

The eucharistic celebration begins with the "Preface," concluding with the "Holy, Holy, Holy" recited by all. The Canon comes next. It is the long eucharistic prayer spoken by the priest. During the Canon the priest recalls the words and acts of Jesus at the Last Supper.

At the key point of the Canon, the priest uses the actual words of Jesus: "This is my body..., this the cup of my blood." It is at this moment, called the *Consecration,* that bread and wine become the body and blood of Christ. The priest holds up the consecrated host and the chalice and asks all to "proclaim the mystery of faith." The response of the people will soon be familiar to you.

The Canon continues with prayers for different groups of people and individuals. It concludes with the priest holding up the body and blood, together. The people recite or sing the "great Amen."

The Lord's Prayer with a long conclusion follows. Then comes the greeting of peace. You simply shake hands with those around you and say, "Peace be with you" or something like it.

My wife was surely happy to learn that the Greeting of Peace is a handshake, not a kiss.

There are people who will ignore you, but their number is dwindling. In many parishes, greetings run forward, backward and to both sides, and the priest and his assistants may join in the handshaking and expressions of Christian warmth.

Communion itself is important enough to merit a separate chapter. It is enough here to indicate what follows Communion: a final prayer, the blessing (to which the people respond by blessing themselves), a word of dismissal and a final hymn. When the longer solemn blessing is used, it is appropriate to answer "Amen" to each of the three parts.

Some Catholics linger to say prayers of thanksgiving after Mass. Often, members of the congregation and the priest pause to talk to one another outside the church. But in every parish there are those who seem to be in a terrible hurry. You may wonder what the urgency is, but after all it does take all kinds to make a parish.

3
Receiving Communion

Catholics believe that Communion is an encounter with Christ himself. This belief is rooted in the New Testament and nurtured by centuries of consistent teaching. In a sense, there is no closer union possible with Christ on this earth than in that unique moment of Communion.

This is not to make Communion an individualist "just Jesus and me" sort of thing. Notice that the word used is "Communion" (rather than simply "union"). The sacrament, in uniting us to Jesus, unites us to each other.

Because Catholics take the matter of Communion so seriously, they often have strong feelings about the way it is administered. It is not unusual for some Catholics to argue that it is more reverent to receive Communion on the tongue than in the hand, or to receive while kneeling rather than standing. Others will argue that standing or receiving in the hand emphasizes the dignity of the Christian. If the issue comes up, you can remind the debaters that at the Last Supper the apostles were probably lying on couches.

This chapter is designed to familiarize you with the Church's rules on Communion and the ways it is administered.

This will leave you free to concentrate on the important thing, the encounter with Jesus himself.

You may already have noticed one difference in terminology. In Protestant churches, people speak of "taking" Communion. Catholics "receive" Communion. The difference is not important, but you can bear it in mind.

Normally Catholics will want to receive Communion at every Mass they attend. The old law against receiving Communion more than once a day has been dropped. Its original purpose was to prevent multiplication of Masses and Communions on the conviction that "more is better" or "you'll get more grace."

Occasionally you will meet a Catholic who insists that you must go to confession every time you go to Communion. Only in cases where you have sinned so seriously as to break your relationship to God are you expected to seek sacramental forgiveness before receiving Communion.

Years ago the Church had a strict law about fasting from midnight before Communion. The law has been gradually modified. Now the only requirement is that you eat or drink nothing but water for an hour before the time of Communion. This presents little difficulty, considering that it takes you some time to get to church, and it takes forty minutes or so of the Mass before Communion is distributed.

Now let us come to the Communion part of the Mass. The priest holds up the consecrated bread, saying, "This is the Lamb of God…" The people answer, "Lord, I am not worthy…" The priest receives Communion first. If Communion is to be given out under the form of bread only, he consumes the contents of the cup or shares it with those who will help in distributing Communion. When the congregation is large, you may see another priest or deacon or specially delegated men and women assist. These are called *ministers of the Eucharist.* A hymn or two may be sung during Communion.

Before going up for Communion, you may want to watch some of the other communicants. You can then see how Communion is administered in this church and at this Mass. There are differences.

There are still a few churches where people kneel for Communion along a Communion rail or the edge of the sanctuary. In this case the minister moves from person to person, then returns to the starting point and begins again. If you stay in the regular flow of traffic, there will be no problem. More often, Communion is received standing. The people form lines and wait their turn to approach one of the ministers who remains in place.

Now we come to the moment of Communion itself. In the United States and in most parts of the world you have some choices. First you can decide whether you want to receive the consecrated bread on the tongue or in the hand. It helps the minister if you signal clearly which you prefer.

The consecrated bread is usually called the *host.* This comes from the Latin *hostia* meaning victim. The Christ present in this bread is the one who offered himself as a sacrificial victim for us on Calvary.

The minister holds up the host and says: "The body of Christ." You reply: "Amen."

If you prefer to receive on the tongue, open your mouth and extend your tongue the way you would when you visit the doctor. The minister places the host on your tongue. You close your mouth and walk away.

Otherwise you extend your hands, one palm placed on top of the other. The minister places the host on your palm. You pick it up with the other hand and place it in your mouth.

Years ago when everyone received Communion on the tongue, there were always a few "snappers." They have been replaced for the most part by the "snatchers," those who suddenly grab the host at any stage of the process.

You can disregard those who tell you it's a sin to bite the host. The Eucharist is food and is meant to be consumed as such.

When Communion is offered under both forms, bread and wine, you can choose not to receive the consecrated wine. Recovering alcoholics, for example, may choose not to. If you decide to receive, get into line. The minister will say: "The blood of Christ." You answer: "Amen," and take the cup into your hands. Take a small sip and hand the cup back to the minister. The minister will wipe the rim and offer it to the next person.

Drinking from the cup expresses well our response to the invitation of Jesus to "take this, all of you, and drink from it." In some places, however, the method of intinction is used. The method works well when everyone receives on the tongue. The minister says: "The body and blood of Christ." You reply: "Amen." The minister dips the host into the cup and puts it on your tongue.

Current liturgical rules oppose intinction when communicants want to dip the host themselves, though this is done in some places. There can be spilling and mess, especially when children are involved.

No matter how Communion is administered—kneeling, standing, sitting at a table—whether it's the tiny white host or a chunk of Syrian bread with a healthy sip of Burgundy wine—it is Jesus you are meeting, it is Jesus who nourishes you and invites you closer to himself and to your fellow Christians. The heart of the matter is the encounter with Jesus. If you find that encounter the rarest of experiences, you are not alone.

4

Receiving Sacramental Forgiveness

Most Catholics do not like to go to confession. Most priests do not enjoy hearing confessions. This general dissatisfaction with the sacrament is one of the reasons why in 1977 a new Rite of Penance replaced the older form. As a result, Catholics are beginning to speak more about the sacrament of reconciliation and less about "going to confession."

You as a new Catholic may have serious reservations about this sacrament, no matter what it's called. It may still seem like a visit to a dentist's chair. Yet surely a merciful God is ever ready to forgive, so why not go to him and save a lot of wear and tear on everybody?

There are some good reasons for the sacrament. Let's start with the experience of human reconciliation. Have you ever broken your friendship with anyone and wanted to restore it? How awkward it is to approach the other person! How should I go about it? What words should I use? How hard it is to admit I was wrong! How can I explain the excuses I used to justify the break? How afraid I am of being rejected! How embarrassing all this is to me and to the other person!

Yet these awkward feelings are the very stuff of human relations. I am real and the other person is real. What a magnificent moment this is! The veneers and superficialities fall off and we reveal ourselves as weak and trembling human beings, seeking love and reconciliation.

The sacrament of reconciliation begins with this basic human experience. After all, our sin is not so much a matter of offending God as it is harming or hurting our fellow human beings. This human dimension of the sacrament is important.

Why a priest then? The priest in this case represents the Church. Our sin may harm certain specific people, but it also hurts the Church. As Christians we are members of a community of faith, in this case the Catholic Church. Our sin gives this community a bad name and harms it in other ways. Thus we need reconciliation with the Church.

Finally, God makes use of this sacrament of reconciliation to reconcile sinners to himself. Such has been the traditional teaching of the Church. "If you forgive the sins of any, they are forgiven" (John 20:23). In this sacrament, then, there is forgiveness and reconciliation with God, with the Church and in some way with our fellow human beings.

This indicates why the Church considers the sacrament fundamental, but it does not make clear how often you should seek sacramental forgiveness. As a new Catholic you might want to celebrate the sacrament before Christmas and Easter and perhaps at other times of the year. How often will depend on two factors: (1) if you find yourself falling into patterns of serious sin, and (2) how helpful you find the sacrament in keeping you oriented toward Christian values.

Catholics used to make a sharp distinction between *mortal* (serious) and *venial* (less serious) sin. The distinction may still be helpful in some cases. However, many Catholics had developed a trivialized or taboo notion of sin. Often there was a list of sins to consult, with mortal and venial sins checked off before confession. Such an attitude is betrayed in statements like: "I think it's all right, but the Church says it's a sin." Sin has become something external to them, something that happens to them, not a freely chosen harmful way of acting.

Sin, especially serious sin, is a pattern of conduct (or, at times, a single action) that reflects a choice of some value other than God or the good of others. We may choose power, wealth, pleasure, ease, success or ego gratification and make it the dominant value of our life. If we have made this choice or are well on the way to doing so, the sacrament of reconciliation is the answer.

Even if you are not drifting into anything this fundamental, you might find confession helpful from time to time. It can aid you to reexamine your way of life, to measure your growth in the love of God and neighbor and to identify any habits of selfishness that may be hindering Christian development. Many Catholics find that the sacrament serves this purpose well.

In addition to the better-known private confession or *rite of individual reconciliation,* there is a communal form of the sacrament. The communal celebration is a church service with hymns, prayers, readings from scripture, a homily and other features. There is a point in the service where people are invited to confess individually. In rare cases where the crowd is too large for the number of priests available, a general confession and absolution conclude the service.

The communal form is part of an effort to restore a community dimension to the sacrament. It gets away from the anonymity, the rigidity and the focusing of communal responsibility on one man, the priest, that were characteristic of the older form of private confession. When the opportunity to participate in a communal penance service is offered, you might want to try it.

There are times when individual confession is best; this merits some discussion. Though it is possible to make an appointment with a priest for confession, most people go at the regularly scheduled hours. You can consult the parish bulletin or call the rectory to find out when these are. It is perfectly acceptable to shop around for a priest who you think will be sympathetic and understanding. The priest who hears your confession is called, oddly enough, the confessor. You are the penitent.

Before confessing, it is helpful to go over in your mind what you want to say. This *examination of conscience* should be a realistic appraisal of your spiritual condition, focusing on sinful habits and on any serious sin committed since your last confession. A proper penitential spirit is evident when you're open and honest about your shortcomings and determined to change for the better.

When confessing, be matter-of-fact and succinct. If you have something serious to confess, you may want to give it emphasis by bringing it up first or last. If your sin is a habitual attitude, such as a consistent hatred for someone, indicate that it is more than a passing feeling. If your sins are specific actions, there is no need to give an absolutely accurate count.

My first confession
must have been very
harrowing for you, eh?

Your concern should be to distinguish isolated instances from repeated patterns.

Here are a few hints on confessing:

1. Confess your own sins, not somebody else's: "You see, Father, my husband drinks…"

2. There is no need to tell a long rambling story: "Father, I was in this bar and in comes this blonde who sits down next to me…"

3. Don't worry about shocking your confessor: "His ears will burn when he hears what I have to say." He's heard it all before.

The New Rite of Penance calls for a setting quite different from the old confessionals. A new reconciliation room has at least these two features: a kneeler and screen for those who prefer to be anonymous, and a chair located in such a way that the person can converse with the priest face to face. There may be a table with a Bible and some other furnishings. When you enter, you simply make the basic choice of kneeling behind the screen or sitting in the chair.

There are still some older churches that do not yet have a reconciliation room and will still be using the old confessionals. Each confessional usually has three enclosed sections in it. The priest sits in the middle enclosure; penitents kneel on either side. An electric light system may help you determine when the sections are occupied. At times a line will form on either side, and penitents are expected to wait their turn.

When a penitent's section is free, you go in and kneel down, closing the door or curtain after you. If the priest is busy with a penitent on the other side, the shutter on your side will be closed. When he finishes, he will open the shutter on your side. A screen or curtain separates you from him. This opening of the shutter is an obvious gesture, and you will know it is time to begin. If it isn't that obvious, the priest will say something to let you know he is ready.

The New Rite of Individual Reconciliation is outlined here for you. Though it may seem highly structured and formal, it is meant to be relaxed and conversational. After preparing yourself beforehand and waiting your turn, if need be, you enter the room or confessional and sit or kneel.

1. *Welcome.* The priest may greet you and you can respond. You both make the sign of the cross, audibly.

2. *God's Word.* At your initiative or the priest's you or he may read a passage of scripture and discuss it together. Passages dealing with the healing or forgiving power of Jesus are preferred. Many priests are not ready for this yet, and you may not be up to it. This part is optional.

3. *Confession.* It's customary to mention how long it has been since your last confession. Feel free to bring up any doubts or questions. The priest is there to help you, not scold you.

4. *The Penance.* In response to your confession, the priest may offer you a word of advice or encouragement. He will ask you to do a penance or satisfaction, a token

prayer or action as an expression of your desire to make amends. If it's a prayer you've never heard of or an action that would be unusually difficult for you, explain this to the priest and he will change it to something else. The penance is not done at this point, but afterward.

5. *Act of Contrition.* At this point you express your sorrow for sin by a prayer. It can be a spontaneous one of your own, or one of the many recommended for the New Rite. You can use the Act of Contrition from the back of this book.

6. *Absolution.* The priest will extend his hand over your head and recite the prayer expressing your forgiveness. It concludes with the sign of the cross. You respond, "Amen."

7. *Conclusion.* The priest gives a pleasant word of farewell and you reply in kind. You walk out knowing that you are really forgiven, that you've made a new start and that, believe it or not, you can look God himself in the eye!

Your First Confession

There are two kinds of first confessions. The first type is that of someone who was baptized in another Christian church. If this is your situation, you know that you make your first confession and profession of faith as part of your admission into the Catholic Church. Where conditional baptism is required (in case of serious doubt as to whether you were baptized before or not), the same confessional procedure is followed.

Some people panic when they learn that this first confession is to cover all sins committed since baptism. If you were baptized as a baby, it means confessing the sins of a lifetime. However, the confession need not be an exhaustive laundry list; only significant things should be mentioned. Confess only what you thought was sinful at the time. Knowledge and insight that came later are not retroactive.

The priest who helped prepare you to become a Catholic can offer you guidance. He may hear your confession himself, or he may make an appointment with another priest for you. In any case, you simply follow the procedure outlined earlier. If the stages of the New Rite seem hopelessly confusing to you, just go in and tell the priest that this is your first confession and that you're in the process of being received into the Church. Let him take it from there. Fingernail biting isn't necessary. The priest is on your side, and he knows how difficult a first confession can be.

The second kind of first confession is that of someone who is received into the Catholic Church by baptism. There is no difficulty here. Since baptism is the primary sacrament for the forgiveness of sin, all sins of your past life are forgiven by this baptism. Sins committed before baptism are never confessed in the sacrament of penance. You may receive your First Communion immediately after baptism.

There is one bit of advice that can be helpful here: Don't wait a very long time before making your first confession. If you keep putting it off, the day may come when you really need it, and it will look like a big, high wall to climb over. If you make your first confession when you have only a few small things to confess, you can be relaxed about it and enjoy the experience.

5
Getting Married

"Two become one body" was the way Jesus described marriage. "Two become frantic" is the way some couples remember their wedding preparations. Marriage is one of the great moments in your life, and you want everything to be just right.

In making your preparations for marriage, include the Church early in your plans. Don't pick a date, rent a hall or send out invitations before you consult the priest. Often a priest has many weddings on his schedule. He may not be able to give your wedding the time and attention it deserves unless you give him adequate notice.

Most dioceses require a four- or even a six-month notice before marriage, so that there will be adequate time for all the preparations.

If You Marry a Catholic

Catholic Church law no longer requires the wedding to take place in the parish of the bride. The groom's parish is acceptable. If you want to be married somewhere else, check this out early to avoid disappointment. This is especially true if you want a place other than a church.

There are guidelines for priests to follow in preparing a couple for a wedding, but practices vary from parish to parish. The priest or pastoral ministers will talk with you, ask questions frankly designed to discourage those who are unready for sacramental marriage and try to find out if there are any foreseeable marital problems. There will be documents to obtain and forms to fill out. Some of this is just the bureaucratic officiousness of any large organization. Part is due to the Church's real concern that you are properly prepared to live a lifetime together. Concern is Christian and appropriate. A lifetime can be a long time.

In most places you will be expected to participate in some organized marriage preparation. It may be called Pre-Cana, Engaged Encounter or something like that. Though a priest and professionals may be present, it is usually led by married couples. Lectures, general sessions, small groups and time for the couple together may be included. It may take place on a weekend, all day Saturday or in a weekly evening series.

The couple will also have several meetings with the priest, though sometimes it may be a deacon or pastoral associate. A professional tool, such as Engaged Couples Inventory (ECI) or FOCUS (Inventory by Archdiocise of Omaha Family Life Office), may be used. These inventories contain a hundred or more statements about marriage and their relationship. An example: "I like the way we settle differences between us." The couple takes the inventory separately, agreeing or disagreeing with each of the statements. Their answers are collated and used as a basis for discussion. This helps the counselor to identify the issues where there is conflict or uncertainty. Time need not be wasted on matters where the couple has their hearts and minds together.

Both of you will be asked to produce a baptismal certificate authenticated within six months of the wedding. For a convert, a certificate of profession of faith with its notation of
non-Catholic baptism is an equivalent. You can get the certificate from the place where you were received into the Church.

Both of you also may be asked to fill out a long questionnaire. The questions cover some commonplace facts, your
understanding of what marriage means, any possible obstacles
(impediments) in Church or civil law and your willingness to
marry free of undue pressure. Often the priest will talk separately with each partner, ask the questions and write down the
responses. You read and sign the questionnaire at the end of the
interview. The priest may ask you to take an oath on the Bible
that what you have said is true. Some priests find the routine a
bit oppressive and settle for their own feeling as to the truth-
fulness of the parties. But even some who find the oath inap-
propriate feel obliged to ask for it.

There is an additional procedure that is quite common.
You may be asked to have one or two people who know you well
(usually your parents) come in to see the priest and fill out
another form. The purpose of the form is to get further testi-
mony to the fact that you are free to marry (i.e., that you have
not already been married to somebody else). As a convert, you
may be reluctant to ask somebody, especially a non-Catholic, to
do this. It may help you to know that the procedure rarely takes
more than five minutes of a witness's time.

The procedures described usually are all that is required.
Occasionally there are special permissions called for or other
matters that take extra time. Some couples want to have a priest

friend from elsewhere come in to do the wedding. Usually this can be arranged easily, but it is wise to ask both the friend and the local priest early. If the priest is from out of state, you will want to find out if your state has any legal requirements that complicate this. You must also have your blood test and obtain the wedding license. State and Church combine to give you quite a workout.

With the red tape behind you, you can get down to what really interests you. The new Catholic marriage rite is a beautiful and flexible one. There are alternate forms of the prayers and blessings, and you have a wide choice of the scripture readings.

You can express your marriage vows without repeating them phrase-by-phrase after the priest if you like. The priest will have a booklet to show you the variety of choices open to you. You can plan with him a ceremony that seems particularly suitable to you.

You may have a wedding with or without a Nuptial Mass. The Nuptial Mass is beautiful and offers you more choices of variables. Most Catholics want it. However, sometimes a convert's family would be uncomfortable with a Mass. Rather than have them feel less than perfectly at home, the convert may choose to have a simple wedding ceremony. Still, by talking over a sticky situation with the priest, you probably can get him to give a brief homily that explains the Mass and makes the non-Catholic family feel welcome.

Usually you can have the kind of music you want at your wedding, even guitars. Often, though, there are diocesan and parish rules on this and other liturgical celebration matters.

Most Catholic weddings are held on Saturdays. This may limit your choice of a wedding time somewhat: Parish Saturday evening Mass and confessions have to be taken into account. There is a standard fee for a wedding, and it is appropriate for you to ask what it is and what it covers. Anything you may wish to give the priest is separate from the standard fee.

A rehearsal is usually held the evening before the wedding. This is a time when it is important to have the full wedding party get to church on time. Otherwise, more than the priest may be delayed. Other rehearsals may be scheduled for the same night. Church law does not require that the two official witnesses (the best man and the maid/matron of honor) be Catholics.

If You Marry a Non-Catholic

If you plan to marry a non-Catholic, the two of you will be expected to make the same preparations that two Catholics would. Special instructions in the Catholic faith for the non-Catholic party, once required, have generally disappeared.

The Catholic party must promise to raise the children as Catholics. The non-Catholic party is no longer asked to do so, but must be informed that the Catholic is making such a promise. Realistically, the religious identity of the children should be thoroughly discussed and settled before beginning the marriage preparations.

You would probably prefer a wedding without a Mass when both families are mostly non-Catholic. An unresponsive, uncomprehending congregation is not the best setting for a

Mass. If you do have a Mass, remember that a non-Catholic, even a bride or groom, is not allowed to receive Communion without special permission of the bishop. This permission is rarely given.

Catholic Church law does not allow two ceremonies, one Catholic and another in some other setting. But a minister or rabbi can be invited to participate in the Catholic wedding service. This is a secondary role, so watch out for sensitivities here.

For a good enough reason, you can get a Catholic Church permission to have the wedding celebrated by a minister or rabbi or even a civil magistrate. This permission is called a *dispensation from form.* The couple is still expected to go through all the usual preparations for a Catholic marriage. A priest can be present at such a ceremony in a secondary role, but this is not required.

The Church takes marriage very seriously. As a result, if you marry outside the Church without getting the necessary permissions, the marriage is not valid in the eyes of the Church.

This chapter has been so procedural that it may obscure something important: Nearly everybody moves through the red tape without significant problems. And the end result is wonderful: a Christian marriage.

6
Buying a Bible

If you don't already own a good Bible, you certainly will want one. Getting the right version is not just a matter of walking into a bookstore and asking for a Bible. The clerk just might go to the back room, find one of a type that doesn't sell, blow off the dust and set you up for a big disappointment.

Bibles come in a variety of translations, covers, sizes, text papers and bindings. Some have many illustrations, often quite colorful. Some editions have expensive leather bindings and gilt-edged pages. The price may be unrelated to the quality of the translation.

If you are buying a Bible to put on display as a very visible symbol of the place of the Word of God in a Christian home, maybe you will want one of the big, expensive editions complete with pages where you can record family births, deaths and marriages. But a book the size of an unabridged dictionary is not very readable. Set in your lap, the volume can cut off the circulation in your legs.

In selecting a Bible for regular use, your first decision is whether you want an old translation or a new one. The King James Bible is a classic of English literature; it is the traditional Bible of English-speaking Protestants. Some people are so used to its phrasing that they can't conceive of a Bible written in modern American English. If this is true of you, you might do well to stay with the King James. Its quaint old-fashioned language is beautiful. But remember that many of the words and phrases have changed their meaning since Shakespeare's time.

One thing is certain: You can do better than the old Catholic version, the Douay. Its language is as quaint as the King James though not quite so beautiful. But its footnotes and explanatory materials are naive and lack the insights of recent Biblical scholarship. You may also want to avoid the translations that came out in the 1940s. The English is better, the explanatory materials are better, but later translations have made significant improvements over these. Catholic versions of the Bibles from the 1940s are labeled (somewhere on the flyleaf) "Confraternity" or "Knox."

Here is a good rule-of-thumb: Pick up a Bible offered to you, open it, leaf through and try to find the word "thou." If you can't find it, you're on the right track. You are holding a Bible that has been enriched by modern scholarship. Watch out for catchy titles like Family Bible, Wedding Bible or Blue Jeans Bible. Look inside to find out which translation it really is.

Another consideration is whether you want a Catholic or a Protestant version. Old fears of "slanting" are now unfounded. The good modern translations are reliable, whether they are Protestant or Catholic. There are still a few sectarian versions circulating, but these are conspicuously full of "thous" and archaic language. You need not hesitate to purchase a modern Protestant Bible if its language and format impress you.

Don't you sell some kind of abridged Bible for beginners?

Two differences still remain between Catholic and Protestant versions. The Catholic list or "canon" of the Old Testament books has several not usually found in Protestant Bibles. These books are: Baruch, Judith, Tobit (Tobias), Wisdom, Sirach (Ecclesiasticus), 1 and 2 Maccabees and the parts of Esther and Daniel originally written in Greek.

The other difference stems from the traditional Protestant emphasis on the Bible as the Word of God presented without comment or interpretation. Protestant Bibles often have no introductory materials. Footnotes usually refer only to possible variations in the original text. Catholic Bibles tend to have a wealth of introductory material and explanatory footnotes.

The Revised Standard Version (RSV) has been the most commonly used Protestant version. It is an honest effort to combine as much of the traditional phrasing as possible with the best of modern scholarship. Many Catholics prefer it for this reason. It was revised in 1989 primarily to make the language more "inclusive." Male-oriented words like "man," "mankind," generic "he" or "his," "brothers" (referring to believers) are replaced by rephrasing the sentence.

In the New Revised Standard Version (NRSV), sometimes a plural replaces the original singular. Take Mark 8:34: "If any man would come after me, let him deny himself and take up his cross and follow me" (RSV). Whereas in the NRSV we have: "If any want to become my followers, let them deny themselves and take up their cross and follow me."

Other modern Protestant versions are now in circulation. The New English Bible is well done, but has a British accent to it. The Good News Bible published by the American Bible

Society has a breezy American style. The Living Bible, an American paraphrase, departs too much from the original to merit consideration. Very popular among evangelical Protestants is the New International Version (NIV); it's quite well done. Some Protestant Bibles, but not all, include the longer list of Old Testament books in a separate section called the Apocrypha.

The two most commonly used modern Catholic translations are the Jerusalem Bible and the New American Bible (NAB). Both are in excellent modern English and both have abundant explanatory materials that reflect the best recent scholarship. The NAB is the version usually read at Mass. Both have been somewhat revised in recent years; the NAB was revised to make it more inclusive, though not as radically as the NRSV.

One last consideration: What about the readability of the edition you propose to buy? Is the print crowded and small? Is the layout of pages a convenient and helpful one? Find an edition that does not weary the eye. Most Bibles come in a variety of editions. Reading a page or two will tell you if you have the right edition of the version that is best for you.

The written Word of God can be an invaluable resource in your life. Whether or not access to that resource is convenient and pleasant will depend on how much care you put into choosing a Bible.

Sometimes it is done as a church service, with the leader moving from station to station and the people remaining in their pews.

A last point of interest is the baptistry. This is usually located near the main doors of the church. It is there to symbolize the entrance of the newly baptized into the Church. The baptistry includes the baptismal font itself and the area around it.

Each church can have distinctive characteristics of its own, and the possibilities are too various to describe. Every diocese has one church that is considered the mother church of the diocese, the bishop's own church. This church is called the cathedral (from the Latin *cathedra*—chair; that is, the bishop's chair).

A church that is famous for its history or devotional appeal may be designated by the Vatican as a *basilica*. A chapel is a place other than a parish church where Mass can be offered regularly. A large church may have a small chapel as a separate part of the building.

Catholics have taken the liturgy everywhere. Masses in the home are not uncommon, and farm workers have had Masses in the fields. Nevertheless, you are likely to attend Mass most often in a church. This chapter will have served its purpose if it helps you to see the common characteristics shared by churches that may differ remarkably in design and decoration.

8

When Someone Is Sick

Jesus offered healing and forgiveness to those who came to him diseased or maimed in body or spirit. The Church continues this same ministry of healing and forgiveness through its pastoral care of the sick.

Most parishes now have an organized pastoral care of the sick. Not only the priest, but also a deacon, those designated as ministers of the Eucharist and even others may be involved. The sick are visited regularly and the sacraments offered when requested. Of course it is necessary for relatives or friends of the sick to notify the parish. The more information the better: the patient's physical condition, age, whether at home or in the hospital, the patient's attitude toward the Church.

In cases of emergency, the priest will come at any hour of the day or night. Emergency sick calls do not involve an elaborate ritual—despite anything misinformed Catholics or outdated books may lead you to believe. For example, there is no need to meet the priest at the door with a lighted candle. In cases of emergency sick calls or the patient's reception of Holy Communion, it is necessary only to have a small table near the patient in clean and uncluttered condition. A fresh glass of water may prove helpful. The priest will bring everything else that is needed.

Pastors and parishioners involved in ministry to the sick will visit their people in the hospitals. However, hospitals usually have a Catholic chaplain, a priest from a nearby parish, who brings the sacraments. Most hospitals ask the patient's religion and make the lists available to the clergy. Catholic priests often hesitate to visit non-Catholic patients unless they are specifically invited. The impression of imposing Catholicism on the sick is worth avoiding.

One of the problems a priest encounters when visiting a patient at home or in the hospital is the attitude of a patient who has been handled badly. Well-meaning relatives sometimes invite a priest to visit a patient who has been away from the sacraments for years and who has no intention of welcoming either the priest or the suggestion of confession. It makes good sense to inform the priest of the real situation so that he can act with sensitivity and understanding.

On his visits the priest is not concerned only with the sacraments of penance and Communion. He can encourage and console the patient and give him a chance to talk about his concerns. Ordinarily the priest will not bring Communion on the first visit. He will want to make sure that the patient is prepared for it. Pastors even have the right to confirm seriously ill parishioners who have missed the sacrament of confirmation.

But the sacrament most helpful to the seriously ill is the anointing of the sick (once called extreme unction). This sacrament has been the focus of superstition and myth. Its meaning can be distorted if there is a shortage of understanding among those concerned. The problem is a holdover from a time when anointing of the sick was widely considered to be the "last rites."

Anointing of the sick should not be considered an immediate preparation for death. So conceived, it may be postponed until the patient has been thoroughly drugged or is in a final coma. Relatives take great care not to frighten the patient. One result of this overprotectiveness can be that the patient loses most of the benefit of the sacrament. The anointing becomes little more than a farewell prayer to console the relatives.

According to the most serious teaching of the Church, the anointing of the sick is intended for anyone who is seriously ill. The Church recognizes the unity of the whole person, spiritual and physical, body and soul. One who is seriously ill may be despondent, feel useless or burdensome to others or feel abandoned by God. The anointing of the sick is intended to heal this spiritual disorder of illness and old age. The spiritual healing power of the sacrament sometimes helps a person to recover physically. Sins can be forgiven through the sacrament. The patient who receives it is in far better condition to face death, should it come.

It is hard to overemphasize the sadness of the game often played by seriously ill patients and their relatives. These patients know they are in critical condition but pretend that they don't know so that their loved ones won't be worried. The relatives know the condition is critical but pretend otherwise so that the patient won't be alarmed. And yet those who love these patients do not really want them deprived of the healing power of the sacrament. Love for the patients is best expressed by getting them spiritual help while they are conscious and capable of taking consolation.

As a new Catholic you are not encumbered with common misunderstandings. If someone you love is ill or very old, you will want to talk to the person to explain the real significance of the anointing. It is time to call the priest after such groundwork is done. It is good for the whole family to be present for the anointing, to join in the prayers and to be as much a part of it as possible.

Communion brought to the sick at the time of anointing is called *viaticum.* It would be ironic to note that viaticum means "food for the journey" if all Christian life were not considered a pilgrimage. This food may nourish further life. If death does come, it will nourish the person who must pass from this life to the next.

An enlightened Catholic will ask for the anointing when he or she is seriously ill, and will take strength from it. Should it be necessary to face death, the sacrament will become an expression of Christian hope. "For since we believe that Jesus died and rose again, even so, through Jesus, God will bring with him those who have died" (1 Thess 4:14).

9
That First Year

Adjusting to a new Church is like adjusting to a new marriage: A lot depends on the individual and on the person's first experiences with the new institution. For some, the period of adjustment is challenging to say the least. For others, it is an easy, natural transition.

If you feel a bit challenged, you may find some general suggestions helpful. There is no ultimate wisdom in this chapter, but you will find simple recommendations based on varied experiences with many converts. You've already had some initiation into Catholic life during the RCIA or instruction program, so you've made a solid beginning.

The first thing to pin down is this: What sort of adjustments are you facing? Those who become Catholics as adults are not a matched set. There are those who have been going to Mass for years, who are quite familiar with Catholic practices and folkways and who already have some connection with a parish community. Then there are those who have hardly been to Mass at all, who find everything strange and different and who wish that there were clearer road signs to guide the Catholic pilgrimage. From wherever you're starting, it will be wise to walk before you run.

If you don't know the simplest prayers like the Hail Mary, start there. Take time to get familiar with the sacraments. If you don't really understand basic doctrines, spend some time reading and trying to make some sense out of them. It may help to discuss troublesome points with informed Catholics or with a congenial priest. If you are already at home in a parish, any involvement with parish organizations should be limited to activities that seem particularly worthwhile to you. First enthusiasm is too good to waste on projects your heart is not in.

It's good to have a counselor or advisor you can see from time to time. It might be the priest or someone else from the RCIA team or your sponsor. Such people can answer questions, clear up misunderstandings and offer some suggestions. They've been part of your spiritual journey and they want to see you continue to progress.

A sacrament you may have missed is confirmation. Current practice calls for confirmation to be administered by the priest immediately after adult baptism or profession of faith. This is true not only of the Easter Vigil, but also at other times of the year. If you are unsure whether you were confirmed or not, ask. Your certificate, if you got one, may indicate this. If not, the parish records or the priest can be consulted.

Confirmation ordinarily is administered by a bishop. If you weren't confirmed when you entered the Church, you probably will want to receive the sacrament before too long. The bishop usually makes the rounds of the parishes for confirmation, but in some places there is a confirmation for adults occasionally in the cathedral of the diocese.

The new rite of confirmation is impressive. Most of your Catholic friends will have experienced a different rite and may not be too helpful in describing what to expect; so, some background follows here. The new rite recommends that you have as your sponsor the same person who sponsored you at baptism or at the profession of faith.

The ceremony emphasizes our dependence on the healing and strengthening power of the Holy Spirit. Confirmation preferably is celebrated in the context of a Mass in which the prayers call on the Holy Spirit to establish its enlivening presence in the persons to be confirmed.

After the reading of the Gospel and the homily, those to be confirmed renew their baptismal vows. The bishop extends his hands over the confirmands praying to the Holy Spirit to be their helper and guide, to give them the spirit of wisdom and understanding, the spirit of right judgment and courage, the spirit of knowledge and love and the spirit of reverence in his service.

The bishop anoints each person individually with chrism, a special oil blessed on Holy Thursday. The sponsor places his or her hand on the candidate's right shoulder and gives the candidate's name to the bishop. (In some places candidates give their own name.) The bishop makes the sign of the cross with chrism on the person's forehead, saying, "[*Candidate's name*], be sealed with the gift of the Holy Spirit." The candidate responds, "Amen." The bishop says, "Peace be with you." The candidate then answers, "And also with you."

If you haven't received confirmation, it will be a renewing experience. It is a sign that you are a committed adult Christian ready to make your personal contribution to the community.

I didn't even know I'd been a pagan until somebody was rude and brought it up today.

Turning to other aspects of your first year as a Catholic, it is not overemphasis to repeat that the first year is a time to concentrate on your own personal religious needs. It is a time to overcome any awkwardness and to develop confidence in yourself in new roles. How long this initial period of adjustment should last depends on you and your own situation.

Yet, you may soon find that your personal growth depends on the support of the community. Few grow religiously by themselves, though holy hermits still turn up. Most Christians draw strength from their fellow Christians. As the community sustains you, you may feel compelled to return the favor. But the development of involvement should be natural, not a pressured transition.

Your contribution to parish life may be influenced by factors that include these two: (1) What are the parish's needs and priorities? and (2) What talents and services are you equipped to contribute? High on nearly every parish's priority list is the religious education of parish children. But Christian concern should not be directed only to the young. You may ask yourself if the continuing religious education of adults is being neglected? Are the old and the sick being cared for? What about the poor? If the neighborhood is changing racially, is the parish response the appropriate Christian response? How are the parish finances? Does the parish seem alive and active, or is it just a scattering of individuals who meet for Mass once a week?

When you have a grasp of the parish needs, you probably will want to find out who is doing something about them. The name of a parish organization is unimportant. The questions are: What people are effectively doing Christian work? What groups do they belong to? If such questions help you decide what group you want to work with, you can be forgiven if you don't want to rush in with a flaming sword and answers to everything. Churchgoers really need challenges, but the most effective work tends to be done by those who can work with imperfect people. Example works better than bare precept in the reform of parish organizations, experience seems to suggest. To avoid fighting inertia, start with a group that is accomplishing something. A group of determined somnambulists might be too much to cope with at first. A period of trial and error may be necessary before you find the best way to contribute your services.

Your perspective as a new Catholic and as a new parishioner can be particularly beneficial. By coming in with a fresh outlook and by raising new questions, you may help a group get out of its rut. As time goes on, you may find that you have leadership abilities. If not, simple competence in something you are suited to is contribution enough.

Your effort to give something of yourself to your parish community will be wasted only in parishes where community has died or never come alive. In a healthy parish, working with committed Christians can be an enlarging, enriching experience.

But don't rush in. Jesus assures us that "No one has greater love than this, to lay down one's life for one's friends" (John 15:13). Nevertheless, your new friends in the parish have not been commissioned by God to kill your Christian enthusiasm by embroiling you in parish activities before you are ready for extensive involvement. For that first year, go at your own pace. The Christian enthusiasm you save may be your own.

10
Coping with Change

You know something about coping with change. You've just become a Catholic. That may have seemed like enough change for you. Maybe you expect to be a little disoriented for quite some time. This book has taken that for granted. This chapter suggests why you can expect the Church to undergo further change. If it leaves you reflecting on the concept, "Life means growth," it's not a wasted chapter.

By now you've met lifelong Catholics who are angry about "the changes." You've met those who are confused and disturbed by the same thing. You've met those who think that the Church has not changed enough. You may have been asked if you are for or against the changes.

What kind of a question is that? After all, you may never have experienced an old Latin Solemn High Mass, leafed through a Baltimore catechism or eaten fish on Friday. Coming into the "new" Church, you escaped old hang-ups.

But you're familiar with problems resulting from change. You've given up old religious ways (or old nonreligious ways), and maybe that wasn't easy. Your adjustment to Catholic liturgy, practices and folkways probably is still going on. You may know something of what the shaken Catholics are going through; you've taken a little shaking yourself.

It is good to sympathize with the shaken. It would be disastrous to fall into their kind of rut. Why raise this point? You've demonstrated your capacity for change. True, but what if some of the things you like best about the Church should change? Would you be terribly unsettled? To answer the question for yourself, consider how people get into religious ruts.

Generally people are not overly fond of change. Average people are average because they seek out a comfortable niche in which to be secure and happy. To be challenged or threatened is not sport for the average man or woman.

There are exceptions to this. Some changes are appreciated and looked forward to. We can hardly wait to graduate from school or to complete military service. We joyfully anticipate a wedding day or a promotion on the job. You yourself undoubtedly looked forward to the day when you became a Catholic. The happy changes may mean a bit of awkwardness and some demanding adjustments, but readiness for the stresses goes with the desire for change.

But change usually doesn't affect people this way. It is a jolt to see old familiar buildings razed. Consider what usually happens when an old neighborhood absorbs a concentration of a new ethnic group. Who likes to see old friends pack up and move away to another state? If we have to move for the sake of a job, we may feel uneasy about "starting life all over."

In different degrees, resistance to change is built-in. We don't like to grow older, to develop chronic ailments, to have to slow down because the body isn't what it used to be. We certainly don't like to see loved ones die and pass out of our lives forever. Maybe we don't like to see a younger and different generation challenging our ideals and prejudices. Maybe we feel threatened by the challenge. Change can be unsettling.

If nothing else is an exception to our disinclination toward change, religion must be. God challenges us to become better, to do better. We remember the self-satisfied Pharisees of the Gospel story and the hard things Jesus said to them. If we don't want to be Pharisees, we won't be seeking a comfortable religious groove. But we are quite capable of settling for a routine of religious practices and a safe lifestyle that will guarantee us a contented life here and eternal happiness hereafter.

This is not to say that Catholicism is a swinging religion. To be a Catholic is to be a religious conservative in certain fundamental respects. The Church has survived almost two thousand years, and we are still reciting ancient creeds. During all those centuries the Church has emphasized continuity and consistency with Jesus' teaching. This kind of conservatism was envisioned by Jesus. He expected the message carried by his disciples to be passed on through the centuries. We have felt the power of Jesus' teaching, and we want to pass on the real thing.

Then where does the trouble come in? It comes when Catholics fail to realize that their religion is like the mustard seed of the Gospel. "He put before them another parable: 'The kingdom of heaven is like a mustard seed that someone took and sowed in his field; it is the smallest of all the seeds, but when it has grown it is the greatest of shrubs and becomes a tree, so that the birds of the air come and make nests in its branches" (Matt 13:31–32).

Christianity started out small, grew vast and is still growing. Over the years cleansing rains and deadening snows have come and gone; the heat of fanaticism and the cold of dogmatism, the winds of reform, the receptive soil and the hard ground of indifference all have had their influence on growth. And birds of every variety have nested in the Church's branches.

But the Church remains rooted in Christ. Still, it is seen differently by different cultures, societies and civilizations. Religious practices and customs devised for one society have faded away as a new society developed. The language once used to express religious truth changed to express the same truth to different people.

The Church does experience periods of calm when things seem to have stabilized. If it settles for inertia, it stagnates. Turmoil, conflict, growth and decline have proved more common than periods of calm. Change is normal.

What makes this particularly difficult for older Catholics to understand is their, by now, faint recollection of a long period of calm and stability. The quiet ended about 1960 with the election of President Kennedy and the coronation of Pope John XXIII. Change came with a rush, as it had throughout the Church's history.

Many Catholics had been led to believe that calm and stability were normal for the Church. Some Catholics saw the Catholic Church as a rock of security and serenity in a fast deteriorating world. This view did not prepare people for the challenge, growth and conflict of the last decades.

This is your special concern only if you are unready for new challenges, growth and unrest. But consider whether or not your resiliency is sufficient. Institutions represent a sustaining continuity for those involved in them for years. Yet, as an institution changes, its people can find themselves involved with a different reality than the one that had made them feel at home. When made to feel uncomfortable, people can look back on a more congenial time and romanticize it as a "golden age." The golden age usually is only one generation in the past; it is the province of those who live in memory, unwilling to meet the challenges of the present. "When I was a boy, things were better…" Change from the folkways of twenty or thirty years ago is decline, a turning from the ideal.

Many Catholics romanticize the religious life of their earlier years, especially because it seemed to be a period of calm and stability. As a new Catholic, you aren't likely to remember the past as a golden age. But if you are not conscious of the problem of the Catholic romanticizers, you eventually might set up the present time as your personal golden age. The period when you became a Catholic, when you struggled to understand, when you made your First Communion, when you first got the Church in perspective, this can become a time in Camelot, an unreal ideal.

Can you imagine yourself some years from now telling your children how beautiful the Catholic Church was when you entered? How you enjoyed a rich liturgy, how beautifully simple the sacraments were then, what great people were straightening out the parishes, how an insightful priest made the Church comprehensible to you. Could you find yourself lamenting the golden touch lost by a more callous generation of Catholics? Hopefully not.

The imaginable does not have to become real. Now is the time to realize that, though your present period of adjustment will end, you must continue to change and grow. Not every change is for the better, but change in the sense of growth is fundamental to Christianity.

You would not have become a Catholic if you didn't want to grow in love: love of God and love of your fellow human beings. Maturing, growing in knowledge and understanding, progress toward wisdom and perfect charity—these are the stuff of Christianity. Life means growth. So, live! And continue to grow.

11
Getting an Annulment

We don't like to think about it and we hope it never happens to you, but sometimes marriages break up. Later on one or both of these parties may want to remarry someone else. But you've heard the Catholic principle: "When you marry, you marry for life." Your marriage vows say, "until death do us part."

Is there anything that can be done? Maybe. You've heard about annulments and are not sure exactly what they are. It's not a divorce, but what is it?

First of all, let's start with the correct term: *declaration of nullity.* This is an official Catholic Church decision that a particular marriage is null. This can be done for a number of reasons. The simplest case is this: Catholics are obliged to marry in a Catholic Church ceremony. Or a Catholic may get a special permission called a *dispensation from form* to be married in a non-Catholic ceremony. If this is not done when one or both parties are Catholic, they marry "outside the Church" and the Church considers that marriage invalid. An annulment of this sort is called a *defect of form.*

More complicated are what are called *formal cases.* This is a situation in which the original couple is presumed to be validly married. One or both parties were Catholic at the time and they married in a Catholic ceremony or with dispensation from form. Or both parties were not Catholic at the time. Contrary to what people say, these marriages are presumed valid by the Church.

In a formal case what happens is that an investigation of the original marriage takes place. Was there present at that time a factor or cluster of factors in the bride or groom that prevented it from being a marriage in the full sense of the word? Were there psychological problems: immaturity, substance abuse, lack of understanding of what the marriage commitment involves? After a careful investigation a diocesan marriage tribunal may declare this marriage invalid and free the parties to marry in the Church. Needless to say, formal cases can take a lot more time and effort.

What to do? Ask. Make an appointment with a local priest or pastoral minister to explore the possibility. Sometimes a priest or minister will shy away from dealing with a complicated case. Persist. If need be, call the diocesan office and ask what to do.

The defect of form case is relatively simple. There will be a questionnaire, baptismal, marriage and divorce documents to obtain. If there are children involved, there must be some guarantee that child support is settled. But basically all that is needed is to prove that you or the other party were Catholic at the time and you married outside the Church.

The formal case is much more complicated. It includes all the above requirements for a defect of form case. But there will be a long questionnaire telling your side of the story including your family history, your former spouse's, courtship, the wedding, the first years and so on. Your former spouse will be invited to tell his or her side of the story, but does not have a veto. You will be asked to provide witnesses who will corroborate your story.

Dioceses differ significantly in the length of time, the cost and the accessibility of the diocesan personnel handling your case. Some people are turned off by the process and give up. I say, stay with it. Even if there is no one on the horizon that you want to marry, get your annulment. If you ever do marry again, you want your Church to be part of it.

Part II

"Have you understood all this?" They answered, "Yes." And he said to them, "Therefore every scribe who has been trained for the kingdom of heaven is like the master of a household who brings out of his treasure what is new and what is old." (Matt 13:51–52)

The Catholic Church is a religious family with deep roots into the past. It lives in the present and looks to the future. We are not surprised that like the householder in the Gospel it brings out of its treasure the old and the new. In this second part of the book we look at many of the old ways: organizations, devotions, practices. These have been with us for a long time. Some are fading, some show extraordinary resiliency. We will also look at the new: movements, ideas, trends. Whether they are the ways of the future or ways that are destined to pass quickly, time will tell. They are with us now.

"Every day's a holy
day with me...."

12
Liturgical Life

The Catholic Church has a calendar that is quite different from the ones you pick up in December. The Church's calendar has moods (seasons), events (holy days) and people (saints). Many of the days are dedicated to particular saints, but this is not the place to learn about two hundred religious heroes or heroines. The important thing is the heart of the liturgical calendar, celebration of the saving work—the life, death and resurrection—of Jesus Christ. Following the biblical path of Jesus throughout the year, the liturgy keeps Catholics aware of Jesus' words and deeds. The liturgy will make more sense to you if you understand its pattern.

The Church year begins with the season of Advent, a period of four weeks that ends with Christmas. The Advent season commemorates the long wait of the human race for its Redeemer, the turbulent history of the Chosen People, especially its prophets, and the role of John the Baptist as the immediate forerunner of Jesus. The mood of Advent is sober but not grim because there is an undercurrent of joyful expectation.

Christmas ushers in a season of joy and hope. During this season the Church commemorates the childhood, public appearance (Epiphany) and baptism of Jesus. The Christmas season lasts just two to three weeks.

The next few weeks have no special significance. The Sundays of this period are simply numbered (for example, Third Sunday in Ordinary Time).

Lent is the most distinctive season of the Church's year. It begins on Ash Wednesday in the seventh week before Easter. Easter is the Sunday after the first full moon after the spring equinox. Since Easter is the focal point of the Church's year, the dates of most significant celebrations vary with it. Lent is thought of as a forty-day period. It is, if you don't count Sundays.

On Ash Wednesday Catholics customarily come to church to receive ashes. The distribution of ashes usually takes place at Mass. The priest or another minister places the ashes on the recipient's forehead in the form of a cross, saying, "Remember that you are dust and unto dust you shall return" or, "Repent and believe the Good News." This grim but popular ceremony sets the tone for the season of Lent.

Lent is a time for consciousness of sin, a season of repentance and personal renewal. On the first Sunday of Lent there is often celebrated the second major stage of the RCIA. This stage, called "election," celebrates the parish's acceptance of the catechumens and candidates as ready to be received into the Church at Easter. As the catechumens enter this intense period of preparation for the sacraments, so too the parishioners are encouraged to make their own journey of renewal, reform or change.

Lent reminds us of the last dark months of Jesus' life when his popular following drifted away and his enemies plotted his downfall. The mood of Lent is serious but not morbid.

On the Fridays of Lent, Catholics are expected to observe the traditional abstinence from meat. Ash Wednesday and Good Friday are days of fasting as well as abstinence. Fasting limits the day's meals to one full meal and two half meals. It is customary for Catholics to "do something extra" for Lent, such as attending weekday Mass, or to "give up something" like smoking, drinking or sweets. Of course, Lent is an appropriate time for the sacrament of reconciliation.

The final week of Lent is the most solemn of the year. It begins with Passion (Palm) Sunday. On this day, at the beginning of the service, palms are distributed to the people and blessed. Often there is a procession. This recalls the brief triumphal entry of Jesus into Jerusalem, when palm leaves were spread in his path. At Mass, the Passion is read (thus the official name of Passion Sunday). Passion comes from the Latin *passio,* meaning suffering, endurance. The Passion is the Gospel account of the suffering, crucifixion and death of Jesus. It is taken from Matthew, Mark or Luke, depending on the lectionary cycle. Usually the Passion is read by three readers, with the congregation joining in. Or it may be done even more dramatically.

The final week of Lent is called Holy Week. It culminates in the *Triduum* (Latin for "three days") that begins with the service of Holy Thursday and ends with the Masses of Easter. On Holy Thursday a special Mass in the evening commemorates the Last Supper and the institution of the Eucharist. Sometimes feet are washed in imitation of Jesus' actions at the Last Supper. On Good Friday there is no Mass. It is replaced by a Liturgical Action that includes special prayers, the reading of the Passion from John, the veneration of the cross and receiving of Communion.

The Easter Vigil, celebrated at any time between sundown on Holy Saturday and sunrise on Easter Sunday, is the high point of the Church's year. This is the celebration at which the catechumens and candidates will ordinarily receive the sacraments of initiation. The service begins usually outside, in darkness. A new fire is begun, the paschal candle is lit from this and the light is passed from person to person as the procession enters the darkened church. This "Passover" from darkness to light, from sadness to joy, symbolizes the victory of Jesus over death by his resurrection. The service can last more than two hours, since there are many more readings and ceremonies, in addition to the baptisms, professions of faith and confirmations.

Easter Sunday begins a season of triumph and gladness, of awareness of forgiveness, salvation and the pledge of eternal life. The Easter season lasts for seven weeks. On the fortieth day after Easter, called the Ascension, there is a special celebration of the return of the risen Jesus to his Father. The Easter season concludes with Pentecost Sunday, a commemoration of the Holy Spirit's coming to the first Christians, an event that inspired them to preach the good news to the whole world.

From Pentecost until the following Advent, there are no major liturgical happenings. The Sundays are numbered and continue the enumeration from before Lent (for example, Fifteenth Sunday in Ordinary Time).

Scattered throughout the year are special commemorations of events in the life of Jesus, Mary and some of the saints. These are called *feasts*. Examples are the feast of the Annunciation on March 25 and the feast of St. Francis of Assisi on October 4. The most significant feasts are called holy days.

Catholics are expected to attend Mass on these days, which vary somewhat from country to country. The holy days celebrated in the United States are:

> Immaculate Conception (December 8)
> Christmas (December 25)
> Mary, the Mother of God (New Year's)
> The Ascension
> Assumption of Mary (August 15)
> All Saints (November 1)

In parts of the country the liturgical celebration of Ascension has been moved to the following Sunday. When certain holy days fall on a Saturday or Monday the obligation is lifted.

The liturgical colors used on the altar vary with the season of the liturgical year or the feast celebrated. This is most noticeable in the color of the Mass vestments. White and gold are used for the Christmas and Easter seasons and for feasts of Jesus, Mary and most saints. Violet is used in Advent and Lent. Red is used on Palm Sunday, Good Friday, Pentecost and on feasts of martyred saints (who shed their blood for the faith). Green is used during Ordinary Time. Violet or white is used at funerals, and white is used at weddings.

Considered all at once, the liturgical cycle seems very complicated. As it is experienced, the cycle will become coherent and simple enough. If you live the liturgical year—share the Church's consciousness of the aspects of Jesus' life celebrated from season to season—you will find yourself naturally oriented toward the life of Jesus and its implications for you.

13
Devotional and Prayer Life

Eucharistic Devotions

Even in private devotional and prayer life, the Eucharist remains primary for Catholics. The custom of making a visit to the Blessed Sacrament has been mentioned earlier in chapter 1. Another custom is that of receiving Communion on the first Friday of the month. A Mass may be offered for the special intention of a particular person; this is most commonly done when someone has died. A monetary offering, called a stipend, is usually given on this occasion. Often these intentions are listed in parish bulletins.

There is the special eucharistic service called *Benediction of the Blessed Sacrament.* In this service the priest takes the large consecrated host from the tabernacle, puts it in a large display vessel called a *monstrance* and sets the monstrance on the altar. Hymns are sung, incense is offered and prayers are recited. Toward the end of the service, the priest blesses the people with the host in the monstrance.

Liturgical changes allowing Mass in the evening have made the Benediction service less prevalent. In some churches, on certain days, the Blessed Sacrament is still "exposed" in the monstrance on the altar for public veneration. Sometimes this is done once a year for a period of forty hours. The Forty-Hours devotion has an opening and a closing ceremony, and during the intervening time various groups keep a vigil in the church. Pope Paul VI abolished the custom of genuflecting on both knees when the Blessed Sacrament is exposed. In some predominantly Catholic countries, the feast of Corpus Christi in June is the occasion for a public procession with the Blessed Sacrament.

Marian Devotions

Next to the Eucharist, devotion to Mary is most popular among Catholics. Most of the medals and cloth badges called *scapulars* that are worn are related to Mary in some way. Some churches have devotional services in honor of Mary. These may run for a period of nine days and are called *novenas*. Often such services are held on the same day of the week throughout the year and are called *perpetual novenas*. May and October are favorite months for Marian devotions. Sometimes a novena is held in honor of the Holy Spirit or one of the saints.

The rosary is the most popular of Marian devotions. Though it may seem dull and repetitious to new Catholics, it need not be if the pattern of meditation on the *mysteries* (events in the lives of Jesus and Mary) is followed.

To say the rosary, this is what you do: On the crucifix say the Apostles' Creed. On the large or isolated bead say the Our Father; on the next three beads say a Hail Mary. On the final bead say the Glory Be. The rest of the rosary is divided into five clusters of ten beads called *decades*. For each decade, say the

Our Father once, the Hail Mary ten times and the Glory Be once. (The steps are outlined below.)

If you'd like to use the pattern of meditating on the traditional mysteries, there are four clusters: the joyful mysteries, the luminous mysteries, the sorrowful mysteries and the glorious mysteries. You can use any cluster you want, but often people use the joyful on Mondays and Thursdays, the sorrowful on Tuesdays and Fridays and the glorious on Wednesdays and Saturdays. On Sundays, you can ordinarily use the glorious, but substitute the joyful in Advent and Christmas, and the sorrowful in Lent. The luminous mysteries may be substituted as well.

1. Make the sign of the cross and say the Apostles' Creed.

2. Say the Our Father.

3. Say three Hail Marys.

4. Say the Glory Be.

5. Announce the First Mystery; then say the Our Father.

6. Say ten Hail Marys.

7. Say the Glory Be.

8. Announce the Second Mystery; then say the Our Father.

9. Repeat 6 and 7.

These are the mysteries, with a text from scripture to help you identify what they are:

Joyful:
    The Annunciation (Luke 1:26–38)
    The Visitation (Luke 1:39–56)

1. Make the Sign of the Cross and say the Apostles Creed.
2. Say the Our Father.
3. Say three Hail Marys.
4. Say the Glory Be to the Father.
5. Announce the First Mystery; then, say the Our Father.
6. Say ten Hail Marys.
7. Say the Glory Be to the Father.
8. Announce the Second Mystery; then, say the Our Father.
    Repeat 6 and 7.

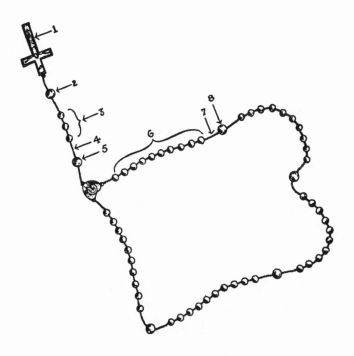

The Nativity (Luke 2:1–20)

The Presentation of the Child Jesus in the Temple (Luke 2:22–39)

The Finding of the Child Jesus in the Temple (Luke 2:41–52)

Luminous:

Jesus' Baptism in the Jordan (Matt 3:13–17)

Jesus' Self-Manifestation at the Wedding of Cana (John 2:1–12)

Jesus' Proclamation of the Kingdom of God with His Call to Conversion (Mark 1:14–15)

The Transfiguration (Luke 9:28–36)

The Institution of the Eucharist, as the Sacramental Expression of the Paschal Mystery (John 22:14–20)

Sorrowful:

The Agony in the Garden (Matt 26:36–46)

The Scourging at the Pillar (John 19:1)

The Crowning with Thorns (John 19:2–6)

The Carrying of the Cross (John 19:16–17)

The Crucifixion and Death of Our Lord (John 19:18–30)

Glorious:

The Resurrection (Matt 28:1–10)

The Ascension (Acts 1:1–11)

The Descent of the Holy Spirit (Acts 2:1–42)

The Assumption of Mary

The Crowning of Mary as Queen of Heaven

The Liturgy of the Hours

More and more laypeople are using the Liturgy of the Hours, the official prayer of the Church. In the past this prayer was available only in Latin and was prayed and sung in monasteries and convents or recited by priests in a four-volume set called the "breviary." Now it's available in English in one volume. The prayer is based on the Psalms and other scriptures and is arranged for the various parts of the day and the liturgical calendar.

Retreats

Most Protestant churches have some kind of spiritual renewal activity periodically. It may be as fundamental as a revival or as sophisticated as a group encounter. Among Catholic activities aimed at spiritual renewal, two stand out: *retreats* and *missions.* For a retreat, a group of people gathers at a place removed from the workaday scene. During a mission, a priest and/or a lay group comes into a parish for a week or two.

Scattered throughout a diocese, often at the edge of a metropolitan area, there are retreat houses. They are usually operated by religious orders. A group of people with some common bond—sometimes they are all teenagers, sometimes single men or women, sometimes married couples, often members of the same parish organization—meet at a retreat house. Usually this is for a weekend (Friday evening to Sunday afternoon), but a retreat can be longer or shorter than that.

The program includes talks by a priest or other qualified people, group discussion, and opportunities for prayer, meditation, confession, counseling or just walking in the woods. Room and board are provided for a modest fee. It is a chance for people to get away for some serious thinking and praying.

Missions

A mission is quite different from a retreat. Its purpose is to revitalize a parish, to renew individual commitment and to move Catholics to think beyond local and individual concerns. Often the mission preacher will speak at all the Masses on a weekend and encourage attendance at the mission events during the coming week. Special sermons, discussions, prayer services, Masses and times for confession will be offered, sometimes aimed at particular groups in a parish. There may be a special theme such as evangelization. Usually missions are led by a priest of a religious order that specializes in this work.

Of course, the word mission has other meanings. There are missionaries in foreign countries working for the spread of Christianity, and in this country a church without a resident priest is technically called a mission. But these usages are beside the point at hand.

Devotional and prayer life are an individual matter. The Mass is the shared essential. How you pray and express devotion outside of the Mass is entirely up to your own needs and preferences.

14
Organizations

Parish-Based Groups

There are two major distinctions in parish organizations. One distinction is between groups that are for men only or women only (the older model) and groups that welcome both. The other distinction is between groups that are based in a single parish and those that include a number of parishes.

In some parishes you may still find catchall men's and women's organizations. For the men there is the Holy Name Society. A monthly Communion Sunday and a breakfast meeting featuring a football coach or other noncontroversial type may be all that bind the group together. For the women there may be something like the Altar and Rosary Society. Sometimes this is just a small group of women who concentrate on care of the sanctuary.

In some parishes you will find the Legion of Mary. Always a small group, the Legion blends Marian devotion with zealous efforts to get "fallen-aways" back to Mass and the sacraments. Most parishes have a St. Vincent de Paul Society that provides a temporary aid to the needy of the parish.

The letters CCD do not designate a federal agency. They refer to the Confraternity of Christian Doctrine. The CCD is an effort to provide Catholic religious education for children who

Join the Ladies' Guild?
That sounds like a union
for
guilded women!

go to public schools. Men and women from the parish serve as teachers, preferably after training by professionals.

The letters CFM stand for the Christian Family Movement. The CFM is an organization of married couples who meet in homes in groups of five to eight couples. The groups discuss scripture, liturgy and the problems of the neighborhood and the wider community. Following a format of "see, judge and act," the groups try to move from discussion to concrete action.

The Knights of Columbus is a men's society organized into councils that draw their membership from an area larger than that of a parish. The Knights were originally organized as an insurance society and as a sort of Catholic counterweight to the Masons. Frequently criticized as being little more than a social club, the Knights in many places do effective Christian work.

In recent years there has been a growing awareness that the typical American family of mother, father and children is not the only group needing parish attention. Many different groups with a variety of titles have sprung up. There are organizations for senior citizens, for the widowed, for singles (either never-married or single parents), for divorced Catholics and for homosexuals. Dignity, for example, is the title of the largest organization for Catholic gays and lesbians, but there are others with different titles. Some other special interest groups will be discussed in chapter 18 on "Movements."

Campus Ministry

Ministry on college and university campuses sometimes uses an organization model, sometimes not. Often the "Newman

Club" model is maintained because the campus ministry's only official access to the school is through a registered student organization. The old Newman model attempted to do three things for Catholic students on secular college campuses:

1. Provide a sanctuary for religious practice and a citadel of orthodoxy in the secular environment.

2. Provide a social club for Catholic students and increase the prospects for Catholic marriages.

3. Serve as "Catholic schools on campus" where Catholic students could take courses in philosophy and theology of a quality equal to academic courses offered at the college.

This was a defensive posture, and it changed particularly with the beginning of the civil rights movement. Catholic chaplains and students began to join Protestants, Jews and secular liberals in espousing the cause of African Americans. It was not the first American Catholic venture into activism, but it came when such a venture was unexpected. It changed the role of the campus ministry and its effects spilled over into the Church at large.

Soon cooperative efforts on campus sent clergy and students of all faiths into the South for protest marches and into the Northern slums for tutoring and community action projects. Other minority groups were recognized and many social injustices began to be called by their right names. The student passivity of the 1950s yielded to the activism of the 1960s, and not without religious leadership. Students of an activist temperament began to crowd tamer students out of the religious centers, to the delight of the chaplains.

At Catholic campus centers, sisters, faculty and professional people formed teams to lead the students to develop mature Christian attitudes and to commit themselves to the struggle for racial and social justice. As time went on, the Vietnam War drew out antiwar activism and encouraged hostility to the military-industrial establishment.

Strong reaction to all this activism came from students and parents who claimed that the spiritual needs of the students were being neglected. The sudden and rapid rise of fundamentalism and the cults with their simple answers and rigid solutions to life's problems added weight to their case. Parents began to beg campus ministers to save their sons and daughters from being turned into "zombies."

Today's campus chaplains are often laypeople or nuns, as well as priests. Even Catholic colleges now have campus ministers. Campus ministers now try to strike a good balance among these three objectives:

1. To help students in their personal growth, spiritual, social and intellectual.

2. To provide a Christian dimension to the university as such: faculty, administration and structures.

3. To stimulate an awareness of the need for social justice and world peace, and a concern for those less fortunate than themselves.

15
When Someone Dies

If your parent, spouse, child or someone you have responsibility for dies, the religious factor needs to be faced. If the deceased is not a Catholic but a member of another faith, you'll need to contact that pastor and work things out from there.

If the deceased is Catholic, however, there is a process to be followed. Years ago the wake and Requiem Mass were all carefully delineated and you needed to do nothing more than set the day and times. Now there are a variety of options. Admittedly you are not in the joyful expectant mood you would be in preparing your wedding. But you will be happy that you overcame your reluctance and helped plan an appropriate departure for your beloved.

First, call the parish, tell them of your need and settle on days and times. Sometimes a funeral director will help you on this. But you or someone in your family will want to talk to the priest or whoever plans the liturgy to express your preferences.

Next, cremate or not? Cremation is now allowed, though the Church prefers that even in this case the body be present at the funeral liturgy. However, there is an alternate service with the cremains present or a memorial Mass without body or cremains.

There are three stages to the Catholic funeral process: the vigil, the funeral liturgy and the graveside. When appropriate, one or two of these can be omitted.

The Vigil

There is a liturgical vigil service for the evening before the funeral service or burial. This can include appropriate words from a relative or friend of the deceased. However you may be confronted by people who are expecting the rosary and a large social gathering. This is an American Catholic social custom called the "wake" which I will describe in detail later.

The Funeral Liturgy

This is almost always a Mass of the Resurrection (formally known as the Mass of Christian Burial) offered by a priest in the church. However it can be a service led by a priest or deacon in the funeral parlor. The Mass calls for three readings, as on Sunday. You have a say in which readings are to be used and in the choice of lector. Though there are liturgical principles involved, you also have a say in what hymns and service music will be used. The priest's sermon is to be a homily on the readings, not a eulogy of the deceased. However there is a place after Communion for a family member or friend to say a few words about the deceased. At the end of the Mass there is a blessing of the body and a final commendation of the deceased.

The Graveside

Procession to the cemetery usually follows. There is a brief service called the Rite of Committal at the graveside. In some large cities, though, this service is held in the cemetery chapel. Arrangements can be made for a burial later or elsewhere, even in a different part of the country.

The Wake

The most distinctive American Catholic social custom is the wake. It grew up originally in Ireland where the time of bereavement was one of the few occasions when occupying British authorities would allow the natives to gather in large numbers. Although the days of great celebration with drinking and conversations to the wee hours of the morning may be over, the wake is still an important part of American Catholic social life. The custom is not confined to the Irish; it is popular with most ethnic Catholic groups.

Wakes are more than a homage to the dead person. They are great gatherings of the clan. Relatives who have not seen or talked to each other for years show up at a wake. As a new Catholic unfamiliar with this custom, you may hesitate to get involved. But if you are married to a born Catholic, you will find no better way to be accepted into the family.

When you enter the funeral parlor, smile and nod but do not try to meet anyone unless another person makes the first move. Go to the front of the room toward the casket. Standing close to the casket are the closest relatives of the deceased. Wait your turn, introduce yourself if you have to and express your condolences.

Then wait your turn if necessary and kneel down at the casket and pray for the deceased. Afterward, another word or two to a close relative is appropriate unless the line of visitors is long. When you are new to the family, usually an older relative will take charge of you and introduce you to all the family members. You do not have to meet the friends and neighbors unless they happen to be talking to a relative.

Wakes used to last for several days. Now they are often reduced to one afternoon and one evening. At the wake on the evening before the funeral the rosary is still sometimes said. But more and more it is being replaced by the newer vigil service. If you have arranged for a Mass to be offered for the deceased, place the card on the table provided for that purpose. Be sure to sign the register; it is a record of those who came to pay their respects.

16
Religious Orders

The variety of Catholic religious orders reflects the diversity of Christian apostolic concerns. Religious orders or communities have sprung up at every stage in the Church's history to meet special needs or crises. The orders are not immune to social pressures, and with time and social change they often become quite different from what their founders intended.

Historically, religious orders began simply. A group of men or women, usually with a forceful leader, felt a need for spiritual growth and closer union with God. They decided to live together and to accept Jesus' invitation to a life of poverty (Matt 19:16–22) and chastity (Matt 19:10–12). They agreed to accept a rule of life and the governance of superior officials, vowing obedience. Often they chose a special task as the work of the order.

If the group or order survived initial difficulties, achieved stability and attracted new members, the order might request to have itself approved and recommended by Rome. A distinctive mode of dress might be adopted, called a *habit*. If the order grew and expanded into new countries, it might make changes in its lifestyle and work.

Wearing a religious
habit has some
compensations.

The oldest order in the Church that has survived to the present day is the Benedictines (sixth century). In the United States there are about 120 orders of men and 400 of women.

Religious orders function as independent entities in the Church. Though subject to Rome, they have their own government, which can be quite democratic. A few small groups are subject to a bishop, but the great majority are independent of the diocesan or parish authority. They make their own arrangements with a bishop or pastor for their services.

Every order has its official title, which may be wordy, and most have a popular nickname. The order to which this author belongs, for example, is officially known as "The Society of Missionary Priests of St. Paul the Apostle." Its nickname is the "Paulists." Members of an order carry a set of initials after their names to identify them by order. The initials can be different from those of the official title or nickname—"C.S.P.," from the Latin "Congregatio Sancti Pauli," are the initials of the Paulist order.

Some religious orders of men are composed entirely of priests and those studying for the priesthood. Others have no priests at all; its members are called brothers. Some orders have both priests and brothers. Monk is a term applied to members of certain orders who are based in monasteries. A monk can be either a priest or a brother.

Members of women's orders are called sisters or nuns or religious. At the present time, the designations are used interchangeably. In the United States sisters have been the main force behind the success of the Catholic schools, but teaching is only one of many specialties pursued by women religious.

More frequently than men's orders, the women's communities get gratuitous advice on how to live their lives. Those who want nuns "to dress like nuns" forget that the traditional habits were originally an adaptation of the costume commonly worn by women at the time the order began.

About 35 percent of the priests in the United States are members of religious orders. The other 65 percent are directly responsible to the various dioceses and are called diocesan or secular priests. The diocesan priests do the bulk of the parish and administrative work of the Church. The priests from the religious orders are more likely to do teaching or some specialized work. Some religious orders have affiliated organizations for laypeople that are sometimes called Third Orders and their members are called tertiaries.

The variety of existing religious orders suggests that Catholic unity is not achieved at the expense of individuality. In a typical diocese like Denver, for example, religious orders of priests are active in many fields. The Jesuits (Society of Jesus) staff a college, a high school, parishes and a prison ministry. Trappists (monks) and the Bethlehem Fathers offer opportunities for retreats. The Capuchin Franciscans operate a large shelter for the homeless and do many other things. For many years the Vincentians administered and taught at a seminary for diocesan candidates for the priesthood. The Paulists do campus ministry through a university parish. Redemptorists and Oblates of Mary Immaculate staff parishes that emphasize Hispanic ministry and do hospital work. Benedictines, Servites, Theatines and the Oblates of St. Francis de Sales add other dimensions to the diocese. Another chapter would be required to list everything done by the sisters and brothers. Of course diocesan priests dominate the parish ministry and do many other things, but a glimpse at the variety of religious orders and their work suggests the diversity present in Catholic unity.

17
In the Parishes

Parish Councils

Before Vatican II the pastor was usually appointed for life. He ran the parish as his own personal domain. Sometimes the assistant priests also had a role in this. But generally the pastor got by with a little help from his friends. Since Vatican II the assistants have become associate pastors, and often the title is not an empty one. Through parish councils the laypeople have gained the opportunity to affect parish policy and programs— but not everywhere.

The parish councils, elected by the parishioners, are designed to establish an official lay structure for the parish. They usually have a governing board and a number of committees responsible for finances, administration of parish property, the parochial school, the religious education of public school children, social service, the liturgy and ecumenism.

Sometimes sisters and priests serve on the parish council. Whether or not the councils work out depends on factors as variable as the pastor's openness, the individual council member's competence, the readiness of the parish community for constructive innovation, the influence of the old guard and so on.

In some places the councils have real responsibility and authority. In others they are simply advisory boards that can be manipulated or ignored by the pastor. The 1983 Code of Canon (Church) Law recommends that a pastoral council be established in every parish, but mandates a finance committee or council. How the two would relate to each other is not yet clear. In any case, the potential of the councils is enormous. They can be a major factor in the development of a responsible laity.

Deacons

Though deacons are a new phenomenon in the parishes, the diaconate is actually an ancient order in the Church, the third level of the Sacrament of Holy Orders (after bishop and priest). Very important in the early Church, the diaconate was allowed to decline into a mere stepping stone on the way to the priesthood.

The Sacrament of Holy Orders gives deacons the right to preach, to baptize, to distribute Holy Communion and to officiate at marriages and funerals. They cannot celebrate the Eucharist, forgive sins or anoint the sick. These sacramental functions are reserved to the priests.

There are two kinds of deacons. Transitional deacons are those who are preparing to become priests and have vowed celibacy. They are ordained to the diaconate a year or so before being ordained priests. Formerly confined to seminary studies for that year, they are now being assigned to parishes as a sort of apprenticeship. They live in the rectory and do a variety of parish tasks.

The second kind of deacon now familiar to Catholics is the diaconate of mature married men authorized by the Second Vatican Council. Catholics who have achieved a proper level of responsibility in their business or professional lives and who have stable marriages can be selected for the diaconate. They are trained for four years in theology and pastoral practice and then ordained as deacons. Originally there were fears that only "safe" men would be accepted into this role and that they would be nothing more than glorified altar boys. Since then deacons have proved their worth and have become an invaluable resource for the Church. May their tribe increase!

Liturgical Roles

It took remarkable liturgical changes to bring you many of the common features of today's Mass. The lector reads the first two passages from the Bible and usually reads the petitions at the Prayer of the Faithful. There is often a leader of song, organist or musicians and a choir. They form the music ministry, while ushers are becoming ministers of hospitality.

A commissioning ceremony is often required before a person becomes an authorized minister of the Eucharist. In some dioceses a distinction is made between those authorized to distribute Communion at Mass (the larger group) and those authorized to bring Communion to the sick (a more select group).

Sometimes one person may take on two or more of these roles at the same Mass, but this is not considered good liturgical practice. Women as well as men are invited to fill all these roles, though this is not true everywhere. The onetime ban on females filling the role of acolyte (server or altar boy) has been lifted.

Baptism of Babies

There is one significant change in the new rite for baptism of infants: The parents take a prominent role, while the role of godparents is diminished. In the ceremony of the past, the priest addressed the child as if he or she was an adult, and the godparents answered for the child. In the new rite the priest questions the parents and godparents about their own faith and their intention to raise the child in the Catholic faith.

Baptism is done in the church, usually on Sundays, often at a regular Sunday Mass. It is still expected that the godparents be Catholic and that the child will be given a saint's name, though there are exceptions to this. Shortly after the child is born (or even beforehand if you like) contact the parish office and find out what is expected in the way of preparations and arrangements. Many parishes have a special program for the parents.

If you would like to have your child baptized somewhere else (for example, back in your old home town where most of your family lives) you will need permission from your own pastor. The pastor back home will also expect you to have taken the baptismal preparations in your own parish before you come.

In emergency cases, a child can be baptized without ceremony. If you can't find a priest or deacon to do it, you can baptize the child yourself. Pour water across the child's forehead while saying, "I baptize you in the name of the Father and of the Son and of the Holy Spirit."

Latest Trends

Large-scale immigration into the United States from all over the world, especially Latin America, the Philippines and Vietnam, has sometimes produced the multicultural parish. In such a parish, Mass may be celebrated in a language other than English on a regular basis. Multilingual liturgies at Christmas and Holy Week and ethnic representation on the parish council, for example, help to unite the parish community.

The declining number of priests has led to a situation where a priest may be pastor of several parishes. Some priests, usually older men, have become sacramental priests, offering Mass and sacraments, but someone else (a deacon, a religious or even a layman or laywoman) will function as the parish administrator. When Mass cannot be provided, a liturgical book, *Sunday Celebrations in the Absence of a Priest,* is used and led by someone trained in the role. This will include a Liturgy of the Word and Communion from hosts consecrated at an earlier Mass.

18
Movements

Beginning in the early 1960s and under the influence of the Second Vatican Council, a variety of *movements* have stirred the American Catholic Church. Movement is a difficult term to define but seems to be the best word here. In this book it means a new emphasis that starts with small groups, grows in numbers and enthusiasm and gradually acquires a national structure to promote it.

Most American Catholics do not participate in these movements, but they have considerable influence. Sometimes they encounter strong opposition from Catholic clergy and people. Often accused of being radical, members of these movements tend to be quite orthodox in their theology, though their activities may be unconventional. Movements find grounds for their particular emphasis in the documents of Vatican II or other official Church pronouncements.

The Cursillo

The earliest of the contemporary Catholic movements is the Cursillo, pronounced "cur-see-yo," meaning "little course." It started in Spain as an effort to instill a strong

Christian commitment in Spanish men. The cursillo was introduced into the United States in Texas and has been adapted to American tastes.

The focus of the movement is the three-day weekend of intense training for leadership that demands more than the conventional retreat. You must be invited to make a cursillo, be eligible to receive the sacraments and be recommended by your pastor. The aim is to attract leaders. Wives may be invited to make a cursillo later, but ordinarily the men must become "cursillistas" first.

The cursillo itself lasts from Thursday evening until Sunday afternoon. It differs from the ordinary retreat that tends to be relaxed and focused on the individual's needs. The coordinator or rector (the lay leader) and his team possess the recommendations and evaluations of each man's pastor and sponsor. Through intense group dynamics they try to draw out a man's strengths and make him face up to his weaknesses.

The cursillo program includes fifteen talks and five meditations. Thursday evening begins with a quiet examination of conscience, continues with a focus on knowledge of the self that extends through all of Friday: Who am I? Saturday is spent in coming to know Christ: Who is Christ? Coming to know Christ in our neighbor is Sunday's theme. The program is avowedly Catholic and heavily sacramental.

The cursillo does not end on Sunday afternoon. It is understood beforehand that participants have made a commitment to a fourth day. They are expected to attend the large group meetings called *ultreya* and smaller meetings of four or five people called reunion groups. Through sharing and mutual reinforcement, cursillistas are motivated toward piety, study and action. Cursillistas are expected to work to Christianize the environment they work and live in.

The Charismatic Renewal

Cursillistas are sometimes attracted to the Charismatic Renewal, but they are not its main inspiration. This movement was originally called the *Catholic Pentecostals* because it was inspired by American Protestant Pentecostals. Since the turn of the last century certain fundamentalist or "Holiness" churches like the Assembly of God and the Church of God (of Cleveland, Tennessee) have been proclaiming a new Pentecost in which the dramatic manifestations of the Holy Spirit described in the New Testament have reappeared in our time. Catholics traditionally have looked down on the Pentecostals, but in the 1960s some Catholics began to see them differently.

They studied the Pentecostals with friendly interest and began to hold small prayer meetings. Soon the charismatic gifts appeared to surface among them. Catholics began to pray in tongues, speak prophecies and interpret them and claimed to experience miracles of spiritual and, at times, physical healing. The movement grew rapidly and has spread throughout the United States and into many other countries.

The weekly prayer meeting is the heart of the Charismatic Renewal. The meetings may be quite small, but often they include hundreds of people. Persons of all ages and backgrounds attend the prayer meetings. Protestants are welcomed. There is much spontaneity, but the leader is expected to maintain a careful control. Unruly elements are not welcomed, and attacks against Catholic doctrine or Church authority are met with a stony silence.

The meetings include singing of hymns, readings from the Bible, personal testimonies to the work of the Spirit in one's life, admonitions to a close personal relationship with Jesus, spontaneous prayers and requests for prayers for various intentions. Charges of mass hysteria and the like, often leveled at the movement in its earlier years, have proved to be entirely unfounded.

Genuinely controversial are the extraordinary manifestations of the Holy Spirit. These include praying in tongues, prophecies and interpretations of prophecies. Praying in tongues begins with expressions of praise in English in low voices from all parts of the room. Someone then begins singing in strange syllables and others join in. It often has a hauntingly beautiful sound, rises in crescendo and then falls.

Prophecies are spoken by one or more individuals in a strange tongue. They are interpreted by other individuals. The interpretations are usually admonitions to prayer and repentance, to acceptance of Jesus and openness to the Spirit. Charismatics are convinced that the tongues and prophecies are spoken in some real ancient or modern language unknown to the speaker, under the direct influence of the Holy Spirit. To others they sound like random syllables of Hebrew or Greek.

A Charismatic community usually has a recognized leader, a small pastoral team and a larger core group. These people may have a smaller prayer meeting at a different time than the general meeting.

Among those who attend the large weekly meetings there are many who drift in and out of the movement, some motivated by curiosity, some by an enthusiasm that wanes. Often a Charismatic community will offer a series called "Life in the Spirit" to explain the movement to newcomers.

Deep suspicions and even hostility of the clergy and other Catholics toward the movement, once very strong, diminished as the renewal moved from the periphery and was absorbed into the mainstream of American Catholic life.

Marriage Encounter

Another movement that began in the 1960s was Marriage Encounter. The era of the 1960s had a strong psychological component. "Becoming a person," being real, honest, authentic, "letting it all hang out" were in the air. It was also the time of the sexual revolution.

Marriage Encounter's fundamental principle is "making a good marriage better." The movement has been deeply involved in developing the theology of marriage, stressing the idea of marriage as a sacrament. In some respects it is like the Cursillo: There is an intense weekend and the expectation that the couple will continue in the movement from then on.

Early in its history, part of the movement broke away under the leadership of Father Chuck Gallagher, S.J. This latter group is called Worldwide Marriage Encounter, the original group National Marriage Encounter. Worldwide is more tightly structured than National.

The weekend is all important. Suitable couples are recruited through parish bulletins and personal contact. A retreat house is rented for the weekend. Various devices, like a clever banner covering the television set, are used to focus all attention on marriage and the couple's relationship, to the exclusion of everything else.

A priest is present—not just any priest, but one who specializes in Marriage Encounter. Most of the presentations, however, are given by married couples, members of the movement. These presentations are carefully prepared and come from the heart, not the head. The weekend is highly structured. Worldwide couples, for example, know exactly what is going on at, say, 11:30 A.M. Saturday at any weekend and they pray for the participants accordingly. There is plenty of opportunity and encouragement for the new couples to speak and express their feelings during the weekend.

Feelings and the communication of these feelings to the partner are crucial. These are stressed so much that the Marriage Encounter literature often uses acronyms such as "HDTMMF" ("How does that make me feel?") or "HDIFA…" ("How do I feel about…?"). To overcome reluctance to express feelings directly, the writing of letters to the spouse is encouraged.

Once the weekend concludes, a time and place are set for the "rookie renewal." This sorts out those couples who are interested in continuing in the movement. Marriage Encounter circles are formed. They meet regularly and sometimes constitute a true base community. Couples use these as a center of social life and commitment to the movement.

Individual couples are encouraged to spend some time each day in fostering their relationship. This will often include written notes expressing their feelings to each other.

Peace and Justice

It was back in 1919 that the American bishops issued their pamphlet entitled "Bishops' Program for Social Reconstruction," a statement on the postwar economy and justice for working people. Historically, however, Catholic activism in this country has been mostly involved in defending the rights of the Catholic minority.

For generations American Catholics tried to prove their loyalty to their country. They volunteered to fight in the nation's wars in higher proportions than others did. They accepted American institutions uncritically, waved the flag enthusiastically and showed that they were 100 percent (or 110 percent) Americans. The cold war following World War II suited all this perfectly. American democracy was in a struggle with an atheistic communism that had enslaved Eastern European countries from which many Catholic immigrants had come.

The turnabout began in the 1960s. Though many Catholics fought courageously in the Vietnam War (many of the anti-Communist Vietnamese were Catholics), a number of others decided that the war was immoral. In company with many other Americans, they refused to serve in the military, burned draft cards and marched in antiwar demonstrations. Some few important Catholic leaders backed this antiwar stance.

During that same decade, the issue of civil rights for African Americans reached its highest intensity. Most American Catholics did not mind seeing priests and nuns involved in demonstrations and marches, even being jailed, in Southern states where few Catholics then lived. But when the struggle moved to the large Northeastern metropolitan centers where the aroused African American minority seemed to pose a threat to the jobs and the neighborhoods of white ethnic Catholics, it was perceived differently. Deep divisions among both clergy and laity separated American Catholics on these issues.

Out of all this history and based on many papal and conciliar documents, a movement of Catholics committed to social justice and efforts for peace began to coalesce. Called *Peace and Justice,* it is treated as a movement because in many ways it is similar to the others discussed. Catholics who are active in these issues tend to form a network of people who know each other, of groups that support one another. These are the people who march in demonstrations, sign the petitions, write to the newspapers and lobby Congress and the legislatures.

On the local or parish level, you see Catholics operating soup kitchens, shelters, and food and clothing banks. There may be a little storefront that provides emergency assistance, counseling and referrals. These places are supported by private donations and church contributions. Sometimes a government agency or United Way may help, but not usually.

On another level you will see a concern for social justice: the rights and needs of minorities, women, senior citizens, and unmarried mothers. At times this will lead to challenges to government policies and practices, employment criteria and the existing legal structure. Life issues are very important: abortion, euthanasia, capital punishment, and gun control, for example. Though, politically, some of these are conservative issues and some are liberal issues, there is a growing concern to respect life all along the line.

This leads to a final life issue: Peace amid the dangers of nuclear war and terrorism. American foreign policy, the military budget and the multiplication of weapons of mass destruction are all causes for concern here. The statements of the American bishops on war and the economy have put peace and justice issues into the mainstream of American Catholic life.

Though all Catholic movements have an ecumenical dimension, people from the Peace and Justice movement are far more likely to form coalitions with other religious and nonreligious groups concerned with the same issue. They have a strong sympathy for the Latin American "theology of liberation." They prefer that American foreign policy take the risk of supporting oppressed people rather than powerful regimes that only serve to create divisions between rich and poor; the powerful and those in need. Their methods and political positions are often opposed by many Catholics. But the issues they deal with touch the lives of almost everyone.

The RCIA

As stated earlier, these letters stand for the Rite of Christian Initiation for Adults. Strictly speaking, the RCIA is a

document issued by Pope Paul VI on January 6, 1972, that insti-
tuted a new liturgical process for the initiation of unbaptized
adults into the Catholic Church. Though new, some of the com-
ponents of this process are ancient. The Rite has begun to
gather around itself a movement of those who feel that it is the
best instrument available for the renewal of the whole parish.

Until well into the 1970s, an unbaptized adult or someone baptized in another church became a Catholic by a much
different process. Often such a person was instructed privately
by a priest. Sometimes a number of such people were gath-
ered into a group called an *inquiry class.* Emphasis was on
understanding and accepting Catholic doctrine. When a person or group was ready, they could be received into the
Church at any time of the year. Usually the baptism or profession of Catholic faith was celebrated apart from the parish's
regular liturgy. Confirmation and sometimes even First
Communion were celebrated later.

The new Rite is quite different. It is parish based and
involves a good number of parishioners in varying roles. There
are a number of liturgical ceremonies and these are almost
always celebrated at Sunday Mass. At least in its final stages,
the Rite is tied down to a particular time of year, culminating
at the Easter Vigil.

The papal document calls for adaptation of the Rite to
local conditions. There is a considerable variation in the way the
RCIA is used. Some parishes make a sharp distinction between
the unbaptized (catechumens) and those baptized in another
church (candidates for full communion); others do not. Often

only parts of the RCIA are in use. Some parishes still use the older instruction method.

A typical pattern for the RCIA would include these elements:

1. *A Pre-Catechumenate or Inquiry Phase.* This phase can begin at any time. September is the most likely. It is a time for gathering information, having questions answered and misunderstandings cleared up.

2. *Catechumenate.* When the inquirers are ready, they can participate in the rite of becoming a catechumen or for those already baptized, the rite of welcoming. This gives them some status in the Catholic Church. As a reminder that they are not fully initiated, catechumens or candidates are often dismissed after the Liturgy of the Word at Sunday Mass and go elsewhere for sharing in the meaning of the day's scriptures. Each catechumen or candidate is given a sponsor as a mentor who has been specially selected. This is a period of spiritual formation and introduction to parish life.

3. *"Election."* On the first Sunday of Lent, the catechumens and candidates who are ready are "elected." The local church declares that they are ready for the sacraments of initiation at Easter. In many dioceses parishes have a "rite of sending." Later in the day the catechumens and candidates, with their sponsors, go to the cathedral or central church to be officially welcomed by the bishop or his delegate. This rite is the first of a series of rites celebrated during Lent, usually

at Sunday Mass, which includes scrutinies, presentations and anointing. Lent is a period of intense preparation for the final initiation at Easter.

4. *Final Initiation.* At the Easter Vigil catechumens are baptized, confirmed and receive their First Communion. Candidates who had been baptized in another church make a profession of Catholic faith, are confirmed and receive their First Communion. These latter will usually have celebrated sacramental reconciliation earlier in the week.

5. *Mystagogia.* During the Easter season the neophytes grow in "understanding the mysteries." They share their new faith experiences with others and take their first hesitant steps as new Catholics.

People who are enthusiastic for the RCIA and its possibilities for renewing the whole parish have some of the characteristics of a movement as described at the beginning of this chapter. A whole parish can make a journey with, and parallel to, that of the catechumens. There can be a learning, questioning phase to begin. A period of spiritual growth can follow, at the time of the catechumenate. Lent can be an intense parish retreat. Holy Week can be a dying to the old and a rising to a better life at Easter. Reflection on all of this can follow.

The parish can start the renewal process all over again the following year. The year just spent may have produced an enthusiastic group of "evangelizers," ready to share their "good news" with others in the coming year.

Others

Sometimes a more formal Evangelization Committee may be formed in a parish to find ways to reach and invite unbelievers to explore the Gospel and the Catholic faith. Considering the fact that the second largest denomination in the United States is that of Catholic dropouts, some formal programs like "Landings" and "Re-Membering Church" can be found to welcome them back. There are also a number of programs focusing on faith sharing in small groups like parish RENEW and Little Rock Scripture Study.

19
Creative Tensions

As a new Catholic, you may find some tensions present in Catholic parish and diocesan life. These tensions are, on the whole, creative ones, encouraging people to stretch their horizons and to welcome a greater diversity (or catholicity!) in the Church.

As a first example, there is the rise in economic status of many Catholics. Not very long ago the great majority of Catholics were blue collar, lower middle class, good, solid people, who had to work hard to make ends meet. Many lived in ethnic neighborhoods. Such people, and there are many still, have their own expectations of what a parish, or pastor, or Catholic school should be.

As many Catholics have become better educated, more affluent, more likely to have moved far from their roots, they have developed a somewhat different set of expectations. Such people often use the parish for their social life, finding there others of like mind and interests. They feel more competent to minister and serve, and thus a variety of ministries and services begin to develop. They often have a great interest in adult education; scripture study is a favorite.

This new flurry of activity is occurring just as the number of priests and religious is diminishing. Priests complain of being overworked, "meetinged out," or having so many sacramental functions that there is no time for anything else. Many parishes have hired religious or laity to be full-time pastoral associates to fill the gap. The educational requirements and other qualifications expected of such associates keep rising, though not necessarily their salaries. They can be caught up in another tension between doing ministry and enabling others to minister.

A different tension in parishes is that of the "normal" family, traditionally the main focus of a parish's ministry, in contrast to the needs of singles (especially those who expect to remain single), the divorced, the widowed, the single parent family and the elderly (who are often far removed from their relatives).

The Catholic school, once the primary tool of ministry in the parish, has undergone considerable change. It can be a source of tension between those who want the school to be the parish's central project, utilizing the resources necessary, and those who want the parish to become more adult-centered and support a variety of other ministries.

The schools do cost quite a bit of money, even though teachers' salaries are low. Sometimes these schools are centralized (made a joint responsibility of several parishes). Non-Catholic children are accepted, usually at full cost. Tuition may keep going up, making it more difficult for parents to afford. All these factors tend to push the school toward the periphery of a parish's concerns, to the distress of those deeply committed to the school.

Another possible source of tension can come from the increased importance of the diocese. Vatican II enhanced dramatically the role of the bishop as focus of the local church.

This has led to a proliferation of diocesan offices, boards, services and gatherings. The diocese can provide resources that a single parish cannot. Parish staff is called upon to fill out questionnaires, make reports and take surveys for the diocese and provide people for diocesan projects.

"Why weren't you there?" is a question frequently addressed to a busy priest, staff member or lay volunteer who has to choose between a parish event and a diocesan one. Striking terror into the hearts of many a pastor is the annual diocesan fund drive. This is done in different ways, but a pastor is expected to meet quota—usually a considerable sum of money. In some dioceses, when a parish does not meet its quota it may have to make up the difference out of regular parish income.

A final source of tension is the pressure to use the Sunday liturgy for purposes other than worship. Second collections are mandated or requested; the priest is asked to "say a few words" in support of each. There is Mission Sunday, Vocations Awareness Week, Pro-Life Month, Thanksgiving Clothing Drive and many, many more. The parish may have its own registration Sunday, or stewardship Sunday. The annual diocesan appeal can stretch out over several Sundays.

To take all these causes seriously and incorporate them into the Sunday Eucharist would make a shambles of the liturgical cycle and three-year lectionary. These causes are all worthwhile, perhaps, but choices have to be made. Tension increases when one cause gets attention and another does not.

This chapter is called "Creative Tensions" because each one of these issues is not an either–or, good guys versus bad guys, issue. Catholics are challenged to stretch, to make room for ideas or needs or causes that you might otherwise ignore.

The fact that so many want to use the Sunday Liturgy for issues highlights the importance of the liturgy. There is a mystery, a transcendence, a real presence there. We come there to pray, to meditate, to experience the divine. But there we are invited to go forth, to share what we have prayed and experienced with others, to be not only "hearers of the word" but "doers" as well.

Appendix

Some Common Prayers

The Sign of the Cross

In the name of the Father, and of the Son, and of the Holy Spirit. Amen.

The Our Father (traditional version)

Our Father, who art in heaven, hallowed be thy name; thy kingdom come; thy will be done on earth as it is in heaven. Give us this day our daily bread; and forgive us our trespasses as we forgive those who trespass against us; and lead us not into temptation, but deliver us from evil. Amen.

The Our Father (new ecumenical version)

Our Father in heaven, holy be your name, your kingdom come, your will be done on earth as in heaven. Give us today our daily bread. Forgive us our sins as we forgive those who sin against us. Do not bring us to the test but deliver us from evil. For the kingdom, the power, and the glory are yours now and forever.

The Hail Mary

Hail Mary, full of grace, the Lord is with you! Blessed are you among women, and blessed is the fruit of your womb, Jesus. Holy Mary, mother of God, pray for us sinners, now and at the hour of our death. Amen.

The Doxology

Glory be to the Father, and to the Son, and to the Holy Spirit, as it was in the beginning, is now, and ever shall be, world without end. Amen.

The Apostles' Creed

I believe in God the Father Almighty, creator of heaven and earth; and in Jesus Christ, his only Son, our Lord; who was conceived by the Holy Spirit, born of the Virgin Mary, suffered under Pontius Pilate, was crucified, died, and was buried. He descended into hell; the third day he arose again from the dead; he ascended into heaven and sits at the right hand of God the Father Almighty; from thence he shall come to judge the living and the dead. I believe in the Holy Spirit, the holy catholic church, the communion of saints, the forgiveness of sins, the resurrection of the body, and life everlasting. Amen.

An Act of Contrition

My God, I am sorry for my sins with all my heart. In choosing to do wrong and failing to do good, I have sinned against you whom I should love above all things. I firmly intend, with your help, to do penance, to sin no more, and to avoid whatever leads me to sin. Our Savior Jesus Christ suffered and died for us. In his name, my God, have mercy.

Grace before Meals

Bless us, O Lord, and these your gifts, which we are about to receive from your bounty, through Christ our Lord. Amen.

Grace after Meals

We give you thanks, O Lord, for all your gifts which we have received from your bounty, through Christ our Lord. Amen.

The Ten Commandments

The full text is found in the Bible in two places: in Exodus 20:1–7 and in Deuteronomy 5:6–21. Christians generally learn an abridged version of these, with slight differences between Catholics and Protestants. This is the arrangement used by Catholics.

1. I am the Lord your God; you shall have no other gods before me.

2. You shall not take the name of the Lord your God in vain.

3. Remember the sabbath day, to keep it holy.

4. Honor your father and your mother.

5. You shall not kill.

6. You shall not commit adultery.

7. You shall not steal.

8. You shall not bear false witness against your neighbor.

9. You shall not covet your neighbor's wife.

10. You shall not covet your neighbor's goods.

The Beatitudes

"Then [Jesus] began to speak, and taught them, saying:

'Blessed are the poor in spirit, for theirs is the kingdom of heaven.

'Blessed are those who mourn, for they will be comforted.

'Blessed are the meek, for they will inherit the earth.

'Blessed are those who hunger and thirst for righteousness, for they will be filled.

'Blessed are the merciful, for they will receive mercy.

'Blessed are the pure in heart, for they will see God.

'Blessed are the peacemakers, for they will be called children of God.

'Blessed are those who are persecuted for righteousness' sake, for theirs is the kingdom of heaven.

'Blessed are you when people revile you and persecute you and utter all kinds of evil against you falsely on my account.

'Rejoice and be glad, for your reward is great in heaven, for in the same way they persecuted the prophets who were before you.'" (Matt 5:2–12)